50 GREAT PUZZLES ON DECLARER PLAY

The bidding is over and you are in the hot seat as declarer. Do you have the techniques to give you the best chance?

Ask yourself these questions every time you are declarer, until the process becomes virtually second nature to you.

How many high-card points are in dummy? How many do you have? Deduct the total from 40. How many points are missing? You might be able to work out the location of the missing points from any opposition bidding or from the early play. How many instant winners do you have? In addition, in a trump contract, how many losers are there? What do you know from the opening lead? Then form a plan of action.

These are the sort of questions that you will face in this book of bridge puzzles. The deals all arose in actual play. Many come from national and international championships. You might be able to do better than declarer did at the table. I know you will tackle the problems with determination and zeal. As a result, your own play is bound to improve with better results at the bridge table, where it counts.

Ron Klinger is a leading international bridge teacher and has represented Australia in many world championships from 1976 to 2016. He has written over sixty books, some of which have been translated into Bulgarian, Chinese, Danish, French, Hebrew and Icelandic. He has written a daily bridge column in *The Sydney Morning Herald* and *The Sun-Herald* from 2002 to 2018. His column now appears only on weekends. He provides constant material for the quizzes and problems on the www.ronklingerbridge.com website and he also contributes to a number of bridge magazines.

T0349793

50 GREAT PUZZLES ON DECLARER PLAY

Ron Klinger

IN ASSOCIATION WITH

PETER CRAWLEY

First published in Great Britain 2019
in association with Peter Crawley
by Weidenfeld & Nicolson
an imprint of the Orion Publishing Group Ltd
Carmelite House, 50 Victoria Embankment, London EC4Y 0DZ

An Hachette UK Company

1 3 5 7 9 10 8 6 4 2

A CIP catalogue record for this book is available from the British Library.

ISBN: 978 1 474 61178 7

Typeset by Modern Bridge Publications
P.O. Box 140, Northbridge NSW 1560, Australia

Printed and bound in Great Britain by
Clays Ltd, Elcograf S.p.A

MIX
Paper from
responsible sources
FSC® C104740

www.orionbooks..co.uk

Contents

Introduction   7

50 Great Puzzles on Declarer Play
and their solutions   9

A Bonus Puzzle   109

Introduction

Do you want to do well at bridge? Practice, practice, practice. Do you want to bring home more contracts? Practice, practice, practice. How can you improve your success as declarer? One technique is by tackling problems on declarer play.

This is not a book to be read through in one sitting. Rather tackle two to four problems daily. There are no set themes. Just as being at the bridge table, you have to deal with each situation as it arises. The puzzles vary in degree of difficulty. If the setting is 'Teams', your objective is not concerned with overtricks, but rather with making your contract or finding the best chance for success. When the setting is 'Pairs', the quest for overtricks can be vital.

In each problem, you are given the auction and the opening lead, plus any early relevant play. Clues for the winning approach may be found in the auction and in the opening lead or the early play. You should try to solve the problem yourself before going to the full deal and the solution on the next page. The answers include the reasoning that would enable you to find the right play.

The deals are not constructed. They arose in actual play and some occurred in national and international events. In many cases, the actual declarer was found wanting. Hopefully you will do better. If you do not find the solutions to every problem, nevertheless the regular exercise will have been good for you. By the end of the book, your declarer skills should definitely have sharpened.

A good idea in an actual tournament is to open this book about 45 minutes before play starts and tackle 4-6 problems. Like an athlete warms up, so you can also warm up your 'little grey cells' and be ready to do your best on the very first board.

Ron Klinger, 2019

1. Teams: Dealer East : Both vulnerable

♠ 10 7 4 3
♡ A 10 9 6 2
◇ A 2
♣ K 4

♠ K J 9 5
♡ Q J 8 5 4
◇ 8 4
♣ A J

West	North	East	South
		1◇	1♡
3◇ (1)	4♡	All pass	

(1) Weak, 0-6 points, 4+ diamonds

West leads the ◇Q. Plan the play.

1. Teams: Dealer East : Both vulnerable

Contract: 4♡
Lead: ◇Q

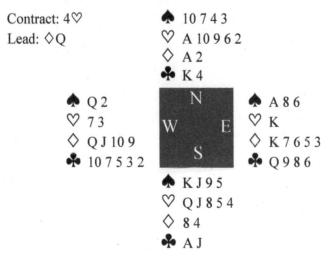

♠ 10 7 4 3
♡ A 10 9 6 2
◇ A 2
♣ K 4

♠ Q 2　　　　　　　　♠ A 8 6
♡ 7 3　　　　　　　　♡ K
◇ Q J 10 9　　　　　◇ K 7 6 5 3
♣ 10 7 5 3 2　　　　♣ Q 9 8 6

♠ K J 9 5
♡ Q J 8 5 4
◇ 8 4
♣ A J

A diamond loser is inevitable and you have finesses in both majors. Which do you take?

In the abstract, the percentage play in hearts is to finesse. It works against ♡K-7, ♡K-3 and ♡K-7-3 with West and costs only when East has the ♡K singleton. However, crossing to the ♣A and taking the heart finesse is not your best move on the actual deal.

West is marked with ◇Q, ◇J and, from the bidding, has at most 6 points. If West does have the ♡K, East will have the ♠A and ♠Q. If you lose a heart to West, you will lose only one spade trick. Therefore, you do not need the heart finesse.

You should take the ◇A and play the ♡A. If the king has not dropped, run the ♠10. If the ♡K does drop, cash the ♡10 and then run the ♠10.

Note that if you take the heart finesse and the layout is as above, you would go down in 4♡. If the spades are as above and East has ♡K-x, 4♡ was always doomed.

Bridge player: One who calls a spade two spades.

2. Teams: Dealer East : Both vulnerable

♠ Q J 8 7 3
♡ Q J 5 4
◇ A 9 3
♣ A

♠ A
♡ A 7 6
◇ K J 10 8 4
♣ K 7 3 2

West	North	East	South
		Pass	1◇
Pass	1♠	Pass	2♣
Pass	2♡ (1)	Pass	2NT
Pass	3NT	All pass	

(1) Fourth suit, forcing to game

West leads the ♣Q. Plan the play.

2. Teams: Dealer East : Both vulnerable

Contract: 3NT
Lead: ♣Q

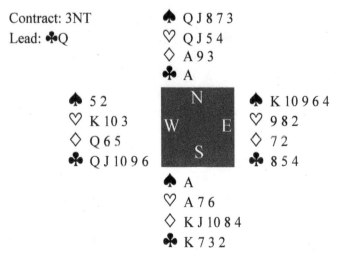

♠ Q J 8 7 3
♡ Q J 5 4
◇ A 9 3
♣ A

♠ 5 2
♡ K 10 3
◇ Q 6 5
♣ Q J 10 9 6

♠ K 10 9 6 4
♡ 9 8 2
◇ 7 2
♣ 8 5 4

♠ A
♡ A 7 6
◇ K J 10 8 4
♣ K 7 3 2

It is tempting to finesse in diamonds next by running the ◇9. That
would be fine if East held the ◇Q, but in practice it is likely to
lead to defeat. West wins and continues clubs. South wins on the
third round but has only eight tricks available. If South crosses to
the ◇A and runs the ♡Q, West wins and cashes clubs. South
loses a heart, a diamond and three clubs.

After winning trick 1, you should take the heart finesse: queen –
two – six – king. West continues clubs and South wins on the third
round. South now leads the ◇J and ducks in dummy if West plays
low. South can afford to lose the diamond to East as long as East
has three clubs or fewer or if the clubs are 4-4. The line
recommended works unless East has the ◇Q and five clubs.

The ♡K is the only entry to West, the probable danger hand and
that should be removed first. You can always prevent West
gaining the lead in diamonds.

Politicians are used to making promises, which they cannot
deliver. Hence they are natural overbidders.

3. Teams: Dealer South : Both vulnerable

North hand:
♠ K Q 10 4
♡ J 10 5 3
♢ Q 8 6 4 3
♣ ---

South hand:
♠ 7 6 2
♡ 9
♢ A K J 10 9
♣ A Q 10 7

West	North	East	South
			1♢
3♣ (1)	4♣ (2)	Pass	5♣ (3)
Pass	5♢	All pass	

(1) Weak, 6+ clubs
(2) Strong diamonds raise
(3) Cue-bid, club control

West leads the ♢7: three – two – ace. Plan the play.

3. Teams: Dealer South : Both vulnerable

Contract: 5◇
Lead: ◇7

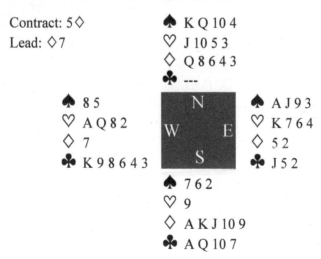

♠ K Q 10 4
♡ J 10 5 3
◇ Q 8 6 4 3
♣ ---

♠ 8 5
♡ A Q 8 2
◇ 7
♣ K 9 8 6 4 3

♠ A J 9 3
♡ K 7 6 4
◇ 5 2
♣ J 5 2

♠ 7 6 2
♡ 9
◇ A K J 10 9
♣ A Q 10 7

North's 4♣ cue-raise of diamonds would not meet with universal support and I would sell all my rights to a bid like West's 3♣ weak jump-overcall for a used 2-cent stamp.

South has a sure loser in hearts and one in spades. Given West's 3♣ bid, East is very likely to have A-J-x or longer in spades. Can you do anything about it? One hope is to set up a heart winner in dummy (with considerable help from the opponents). Another possibility is to create a second club winner. If neither of those produce success, you can fall back on finessing the ♠10.

Declarer crossed to the ◇Q to draw the last trump and played the ♡3: four – nine – queen. West switched to the ♠8: king – ace – two. East returned the ♡6 and South ruffed. Next came the ♣A, discarding the ♠4 from dummy, followed by the ♣7, ruffed in dummy. After another heart ruff, South played the ♣Q: king – ◇6 – ♣J. South ruffed dummy's last heart and played the ♣10, now high, to discard dummy's ♠10 and had eleven tricks.

Bridge definition: 'Opponents': The other three players.

4. Teams: Dealer South : North-South vulnerable

♠ A 9 4 3
♡ 6 5 2
◇ 7 5 3 2
♣ A 8

♠ Q 5
♡ A Q 4
◇ ---
♣ Q J 10 9 6 4 3 2

West	North	East	South
			5♣
Pass	Pass	Pass	

West leads the ◇K: two – four – ♣2. Plan the play.

4. Teams: Dealer South : North-South vulnerable

Contract: 5♣
Lead: ◇K

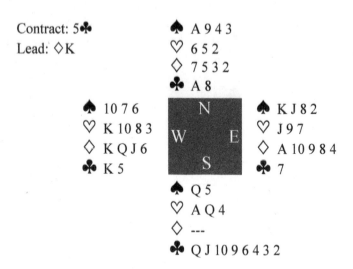

♠ A 9 4 3
♡ 6 5 2
◇ 7 5 3 2
♣ A 8

♠ 10 7 6
♡ K 10 8 3
◇ K Q J 6
♣ K 5

♠ K J 8 2
♡ J 9 7
◇ A 10 9 8 4
♣ 7

♠ Q 5
♡ A Q 4
◇ ---
♣ Q J 10 9 6 4 3 2

If you bid like this, you will need to play well and also have a healthy dose of luck. As you have a spade loser and a heart loser, you cannot afford a club loser. With ten trumps missing the king, the percentage play is to finesse in clubs. The ♣K-7 or ♣K-5 with West is twice as likely as the bare ♣K with East.

The ♠Q is a potentially useful asset. At trick 2, play a low club and finesse the ♣8. Phew! That hurdle is over. Now play a low spade. If East plays low, play the ♠Q. If this loses to West, cross to the ♣A later and take the heart finesse. If the ♠Q wins, you are home. Cross to the ♣A and finesse the ♡Q to try for an overtrick.

In practice, East will rise with the ♠K and switch to a heart. Take the ♡A, cash the ♠Q, cross to the ♣A and discard a heart on the ♠A for eleven tricks. Beware. When East switches to a heart, do not finesse the ♡Q. West wins and can play the ♣K to knock out your outside entry to dummy with the spades still blocked.

"Do you believe in clubs for men?"
"Only if reasoning with them fails."

5. Teams: Dealer West : North-South vulnerable

                     ♠ Q 3
                     ♡ A Q 4 3 2
                     ◇ K J 8 7 6
                     ♣ A

                     ♠ A K 2
                     ♡ 10 7
                     ◇ Q 10 9 5 4 2
                     ♣ J 4

West	North	East	South
Pass	1♡	Pass	2◇
Pass	4◇	Pass	4♠ (1)
Pass	4NT	Pass	5◇ (2)
Pass	6◇	All pass	

(1) Cue-bid, diamonds agreed
(2) One key card for diamonds

West leads the ♣10. Plan the play.

5. Teams: Dealer West : North-South vulnerable

Contract: 6♢
Lead: ♣10

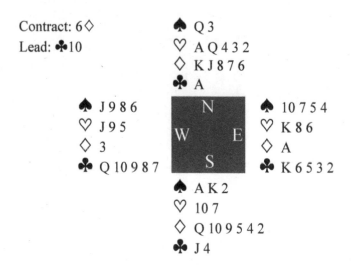

♠ Q 3
♡ A Q 4 3 2
♢ K J 8 7 6
♣ A

♠ J 9 8 6
♡ J 9 5
♢ 3
♣ Q 10 9 8 7

♠ 10 7 5 4
♡ K 8 6
♢ A
♣ K 6 5 3 2

♠ A K 2
♡ 10 7
♢ Q 10 9 5 4 2
♣ J 4

One can fall back on the heart finesse, but that should be a last resort. When the ♢A is singleton with East, you might be able to make your contract without requiring the heart finesse.

Take the ♣A, play the ♠3 to the ♠A and ruff the ♣J. Continue with the ♠Q and overtake it with the ♠K. Ruff the ♠2. With the spades and the clubs eliminated, lead a diamond from dummy. When East wins, there is no successful return. A heart goes into the A-Q and a black suit allows South to discard a heart and ruff in dummy,

Not quite as good is ♣A, ♠Q, ♠K, ♠A, club ruff. East might be able to ruff the third spade with the ♢3. That line would be necessary if West had led a spade.

To defeat 6♢, West needed to lead a trump or a heart. East could have doubled (Lightner) for a heart lead, but that could backfire if South began with a singleton heart and dummy had two clubs.

There are two theories about arguing with your bridge partner. Neither works.

6. Teams: Dealer South : East-West vulnerable

♠ Q J 10 2
♡ 9 8 4
◇ J 5 3
♣ Q 9 8

```
        N
    W       E
        S
```

♠ A K
♡ A K 3 2
◇ A 7 6 4
♣ A J 5

West	North	East	South
			2NT
Pass	3♣ (1)	Pass	3◇ (2)
Pass	3♡ (3)	Pass	3NT (4)
Pass	Pass	Pass	

(1) Puppet Stayman, asking for a 5-card major
(2) No 5-card major
(3) Shows four spades
(4) Does not have four spades

West leads the ♣4: nine – ten from East. Plan the play.

6. Teams: Dealer South : East-West vulnerable

Contract: 3NT
Lead: ♣4

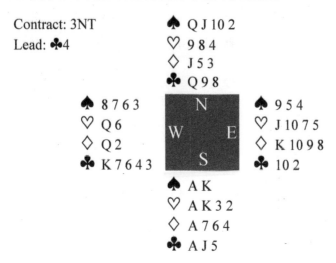

You have nine tricks with four spades, two hearts, one diamond and two clubs. The snag is that the spade suit is blocked. You need an entry to dummy after unblocking the spades. As dummy's only possible entry is in clubs, you must take care at trick 1.

If you win trick 1 cheaply with the ♣J, you cannot be sure of an entry to dummy. If you play ♠A, ♠K and then the ♣5, West can thwart your plan by rising with the ♣K and playing another club, which you have to win with the ♣A.

Take East's ♣10 with the ♣A, cash ♠A, ♠K, and then play the ♣5 to dummy's ♣9 (if West plays low) or the ♣J to dummy's ♣Q (if West plays low). No matter which opponent has the ♣K, you are sure to reach the spade winners in dummy.

If dummy's clubs were Q-6-2, you should still capture East's ♣10 with the ♣A, cash ♠A and ♠K and then lead the ♣5 to the ♣Q. Your hope then is that West began with the ♣K.

'Smother play': *A very attractive move to be used against partner after each session.*

7. Teams: Dealer South : Both vulnerable

♠ K 10 2
♡ A 9 8 5 3
♢ A K
♣ 9 8 2

♠ A J 3
♡ K Q 7 4 2
♢ Q 2
♣ A K J

West	North	East	South
			2NT
Pass	3♢ (1)	Pass	3♡
Pass	5NT (2)	Pass	6♡
Pass	Pass	Pass	

(1) Transfer to hearts
(2) Pick a slam

West leads the ♢ 10. Plan the play.

7. Teams: Dealer South : Both vulnerable

Contract: 6♡
Lead: ◇10

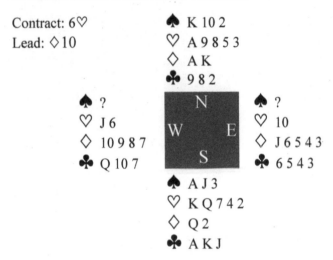

♠ K 10 2
♡ A 9 8 5 3
◇ A K
♣ 9 8 2

♠ ?
♡ J 6
◇ 10 9 8 7
♣ Q 10 7

♠ ?
♡ 10
◇ J 6 5 4 3
♣ 6 5 4 3

♠ A J 3
♡ K Q 7 4 2
◇ Q 2
♣ A K J

You have no losers in the red suits. Finessing the ♣J gives you a 50% chance of success. If that fails, you have a 50% chance of taking a winning finesse, one way or the other, in spades. Total chance of success = about 75%. Good odds? Yes, but why settle for 75%, when there is 100% sure line of play?

Take the ◇A, draw trumps (three rounds if necessary), cash the ◇K, ♣A, ♣K and exit with the ♣J. You now have a void in both hands in diamonds and in clubs and the opponents have no more hearts. Whoever wins the third club will either give you a ruff-and-discard or lead a spade. Either way you have no spade loser and you have eliminated any guess in spades.

What happened to the bashful declarer in 6 ♡? He was two shy.

8. Teams: Dealer South : Nil vulnerable

♠ K 9 8
♡ J 8 4
◇ K Q J 9 8 6
♣ 5

♠ A 5 2
♡ A 10 7 3
◇ A 2
♣ K J 10 8

West	North	East	South
			1NT (1)
Pass	2♣ (2)	Pass	2◇ (3)
Pass	3NT	All pass	

(1) 15-17 points
(2) 5-card major Stayman
(3) No 5-card major

West leads the ◇4: six – ♣6 (discouraging clubs) . . .
Plan the play.

Suppose you choose to win with the ◇A, finesse the ◇9 and
continue with four more diamonds. You discard the ♠2 and ♣8,
♣10, ♣J. West follows to five diamonds, of course, and discards
the ♠7. East discards three more clubs, then the ♠4 and ♠6. Next
you lead the ♡J: king – ace – queen! What now?

8. Teams: Dealer South : Nil vulnerable

Contract: 3NT
Lead: ◇4

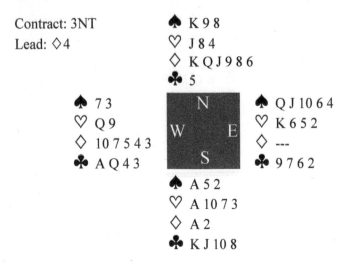

♠ K 9 8
♡ J 8 4
◇ K Q J 9 8 6
♣ 5

♠ 7 3
♡ Q 9
◇ 10 7 5 4 3
♣ A Q 4 3

♠ Q J 10 6 4
♡ K 6 5 2
◇ ---
♣ 9 7 6 2

♠ A 5 2
♡ A 10 7 3
◇ A 2
♣ K J 10 8

You have nine tricks on top, but it does not hurt to play for an overtrick or two if it cannot cost.

When the ◇6 wins in dummy, it cannot cost to play low from hand and then finesse the ♣J, losing to West. If West switches to the ♡Q or a spade, you win with your ace and play the ♣10. This gives you ten tricks at no risk.

When declarer cashed six diamonds first, pitching three clubs and a spade from hand, he continued with the ♡J: king – ace – queen. South can still play for overtricks, but should cash the ♠A and cross to the ♠K. That gives South nine tricks before playing another heart.

West's clever ♡Q from Q-9 completely fooled South, who crossed to the ♠K (without cashing the ♠A first) and played the ♡4: six – seven – nine. West now cashed four clubs and so the 'cold' 3NT was one down.

To err is human; to forgive a bridge partner is highly unlikely.

9. Teams: Dealer East : East-West vulnerable

♠ A Q 3
♥ K 9 8 3
♦ A Q 6 4
♣ 8 6

♠ 7 6
♥ A Q J 10 7
♦ 10 9 3
♣ A 7 5

West	North	East	South
		Pass	1♥
Pass	2NT (1)	Pass	4♥ (2)
Pass	Pass	Pass	

(1) Game-force, 4+ hearts
(2) Minimum opening, no short suit

West leads the ♣K. Plan the play. If you duck, West switches to the ♠9. Trumps turn out to be 2-2.

9. Teams: Dealer East : East-West vulnerable

Contract: 4♡
Lead: ♣K

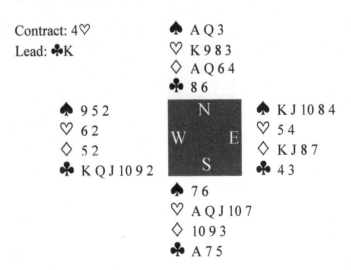

        ♠ A Q 3
        ♡ K 9 8 3
        ◇ A Q 6 4
        ♣ 8 6

♠ 9 5 2   ♠ K J 10 8 4
♡ 6 2   ♡ 5 4
◇ 5 2   ◇ K J 8 7
♣ K Q J 10 9 2   ♣ 4 3

        ♠ 7 6
        ♡ A Q J 10 7
        ◇ 10 9 3
        ♣ A 7 5

In a National Team Selection, most declarers won the ♣K lead, drew trumps, lost a diamond finesse. East returned a club to West, who switched to the ♠9, queen, king. East returned the ♠J. When declarer took a second diamond finesse, that lost, too, and so 4♡ was one down, with three out of three finesses failing.

With such good trump pips, one can do better. One successful line is ♣A and return a club. If West switches to the ♠9, you can finesse the ♠Q. East wins and returns the ♠J, Take the ♠A, ruff the ♣3, ruff your third club with one of dummy's high trumps and then play ♡K, ♡A (and the ♡Q if it were necessary). Now you can run the ◇10 or finesse the ◇Q. East wins but is endplayed. A spade return allows you to ruff in dummy and pitch a diamond from hand, while a diamond return eliminates a loser, too.

Neology: Opportunimist: One who missed his opportunities.

10. Teams: Dealer East : Both vulnerable

♠ A 9 6 4 3
♡ A J 6 4
◇ K 10
♣ Q 2

♠ Q 8
♡ Q 9 8 7 3 2
◇ A J 4 2
♣ 10

West	North	East	South
		1♣	1♡
Pass	2♣ (1)	Double (2)	2◇ (3)
Pass	4♡	All pass	

(1) Strong hand with heart support
(2) Strong clubs, asking for a club lead
(3) Natural, mild try for game

West leads the ♠J. What do you play from dummy?

It is highly unlikely that this is a singleton. That would give East five spades and yet East opened 1♣.

You play low in dummy and East wins with the ♠K. East returns the ♠5: queen – two – four. What is the spade position? How do you plan the play?

10. Teams: Dealer East : Both vulnerable

Contract: 4 ♡
Lead: ♠J

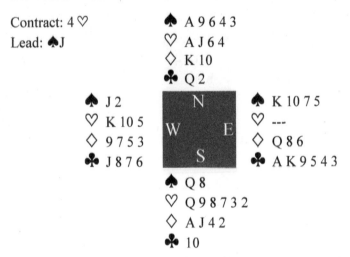

```
                    ♠ A 9 6 4 3
                    ♡ A J 6 4
                    ◇ K 10
                    ♣ Q 2
  ♠ J 2                              ♠ K 10 7 5
  ♡ K 10 5          N               ♡ ---
  ◇ 9 7 5 3      W     E            ◇ Q 8 6
  ♣ J 8 7 6         S               ♣ A K 9 5 4 3
                    ♠ Q 8
                    ♡ Q 9 8 7 3 2
                    ◇ A J 4 2
                    ♣ 10
```

West's ♠J could be J-2 doubleton or from J-10-2 or J-10-7-2, but as West ignored East's request to lead a club, it is likely that West has length in clubs and is seeking a spade ruff.

You can succeed via ♡A and ♠A, discarding ♣10. West can ruff and cash ♡K, but you have the rest. Although not safe, it works to lead the ♡Q and let it run if West plays low. If West covers, take the ♡A, cross to the ◇A and finesse (twice if necessary) against West's ♡10. After drawing trumps, you have twelve tricks.

Running the ♡Q is not safe. It could lose to East's bare ♡K. East could cash a club and play a spade for West to ruff with the ♡10.

What you must not play is a heart to the ace and a heart back. West takes the ♡J or ♡Q, plays a club to East and now a spade sets up West's ♡10 for the fourth trick for the defence.

Bridge writers bid, play and defend all hands with 20-20 vision.

11. Pairs: Dealer South : Nil vulnerable

♠ A 10 8 4
♡ 9 7 6
◇ 6
♣ Q 10 9 8 7

♠ Q 7
♡ A Q J 10 8 5 4 2
◇ 8 3
♣ J

West	North	East	South
			4♡
Double (1)	Pass	5◇	Pass
Pass	5♡	Pass	Pass
Double	Pass	Pass	Pass
(1) For takeout			

West leads the ♣A: seven – two (discouraging) – jack, followed by the ◇A and the ◇K, ruffed with the ♡6. Plan the play.

11. Pairs: Dealer South : Nil vulnerable

Contract: 5♡ doubled
Lead: ♣A

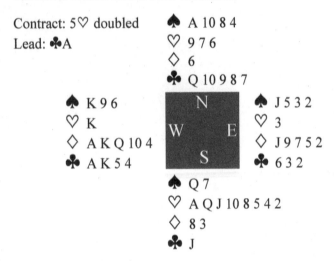

```
                    ♠ A 10 8 4
                    ♡ 9 7 6
                    ◇ 6
                    ♣ Q 10 9 8 7
  ♠ K 9 6             N              ♠ J 5 3 2
  ♡ K                                ♡ 3
  ◇ A K Q 10 4     W     E           ◇ J 9 7 5 2
  ♣ A K 5 4           S              ♣ 6 3 2
                    ♠ Q 7
                    ♡ A Q J 10 8 5 4 2
                    ◇ 8 3
                    ♣ J
```

North felt there was little defence against 5◇, but that was wrong. The defence should take 5◇ two down at least.

One down doubled in 5♡ will be a terrible score. Making will be outstanding. With ◇A-K and ♣A only, West would lead ◇A at trick 1 and so ♣A, ♣K are with West. With ♠K, too, quite likely for the takeout double, West could be in deep trouble in the play.

After ruffing the ◇K, should you finesse in hearts or play ♡A? A 1-1 heart split (52%) is slightly more likely than a 2-0 split. Also, with ♡K-x, East might have doubled 5♡. You play ♡A and when the ♡K drops, you play out the hearts. With one heart left, you hold ♠Q-7, ♡2, dummy has ♠A-10, ♣Q and West is down to ♠K-9, ♣K. On the last trump, West must find a discard. If West throws ♣K, you pitch dummy's ♠10 and dummy is high. If West ditches the ♠9, you discard dummy's ♣Q. After ♠7, king, ace and the ♠10 to your ♠Q, you have made 5♡ doubled. Spare a thought for poor West, 22 HCP and unable to take three tricks.

Drink for bridge players: Freshly squeezed opponent.

12. Pairs: Dealer West : Nil vulnerable

    ♠ K Q 7 6 5 2
    ♡ 5 4 2
    ◇ 8 4
    ♣ 8 3

    ♠ A J 10 9 4
    ♡ K
    ◇ Q 7 2
    ♣ A Q 10 2

West	North	East	South
Pass	Pass	Pass	1♠
2♡	4♠	5♡	5♠
Pass	Pass	Pass	

West leads the ♠3. Plan the play.

12. Pairs: Dealer West : Nil vulnerable

Contract: 5♠
Lead: ♠3

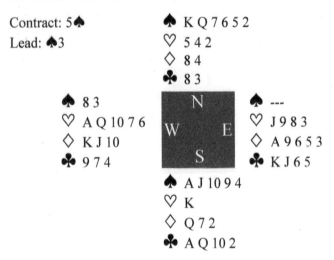

♠ K Q 7 6 5 2
♡ 5 4 2
◇ 8 4
♣ 8 3

♠ 8 3
♡ A Q 10 7 6
◇ K J 10
♣ 9 7 4

♠ ---
♡ J 9 8 3
◇ A 9 6 5 3
♣ K J 6 5

♠ A J 10 9 4
♡ K
◇ Q 7 2
♣ A Q 10 2

It looks strange to bid 5-over-5 when the opponents who have bid
to 5♡ are both passed hands. However, on the actual layout,
North must lead a club to beat 5♡. Why should North find that?
On the normal ♠K lead, West makes eleven tricks easily and
safely by ruffing the spade lead and playing a trump, king, ace.
After ruffing another spade, West draws trumps and plays ◇K
and runs the ◇J to South's ◇Q. The defence can take only a club
and a diamond. A risky line (ruff spade, heart to the ace, spade
ruff, low diamond from dummy to ◇J) gives West twelve tricks.

In 5♣, you are lucky the opponents have not cashed a heart and
two diamonds at once. Your only shot to make 5♠ is via two club
finesses. Take ♠A, cross to ♠K and finesse ♣10. When it wins,
return to dummy with a spade and finesse the ♣Q. When that
wins, discard a diamond from dummy on the ♣A and lead either
red suit. You lose only one heart and one diamond. If you were in
4♠, draw trumps and finesse ♣Q. You need not finesse the ♣10.

Great achievement is usually born of great sacrifice . . .
(Napoleon Hill)

13. Pairs: Dealer West : Both vulnerable

♠ 10 7 6 4 2
♡ K J 5 3
◇ 9 4
♣ K 6

♠ A
♡ A Q 6
◇ A Q J 10 6 2
♣ Q 5 4

West	North	East	South
1♠	Pass	Pass	3NT
Pass	Pass	Pass	

West leads the ♡10. Plan the play.

13. Pairs: Dealer West : Both vulnerable

Contract: 3NT
Lead: ♡10

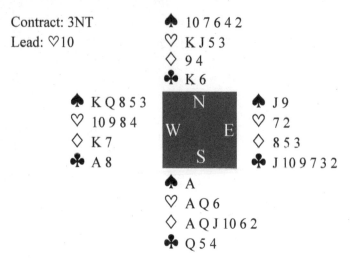

♠ 10 7 6 4 2
♡ K J 5 3
♢ 9 4
♣ K 6

♠ K Q 8 5 3
♡ 10 9 8 4
♢ K 7
♣ A 8

♠ J 9
♡ 7 2
♢ 8 5 3
♣ J 10 9 7 3 2

♠ A
♡ A Q 6
♢ A Q J 10 6 2
♣ Q 5 4

You and dummy have 26 HCP. Of the remaining 14, West figures to have almost all of them, including ♢K and ♣A. As West did not lead a top spade, West's spades will not be headed by K-Q-J.

You could win ♡A and lead a low diamond, hoping West will duck with K-x. Still, West is unlikely to risk losing the ♢K. You could win ♡A and lay down ♢A, followed by ♢Q. This gives you six diamond tricks if West has the ♢K singleton.

A very strong chance for a top board is to win ♡A and lead ♣4. This risks West taking the ♣A and switching to a low spade. That will hold you to nine tricks. However, where West might not duck with ♢K-x, West probably will duck with ♣A-x. When the ♣K wins, you can play ♢A and ♢Q. You now make eleven tricks.

Even if West takes the ♣A, West will probably not switch to a spade, lest South started with ♠A-J. The risk of making only nine tricks is very small and the play of a low club will probably see West play low and you will make 11 tricks for an excellent score.

Food for bridge players: Duck.

14. Teams: Dealer South : Both vulnerable

♠ K J 10 8
♡ A 4
♢ A 8
♣ A K J 9 8

♠ 9 3 2
♡ Q 9 8
♢ K Q J 10 9 7 3
♣ ---

West	North	East	South
			Pass
Pass	1♣	Pass	1♢
Pass	2NT (1)	Pass	6♢
Pass	Pass	Pass	

(1) 18-20 balanced

Some might prefer a 2NT opening for North or 1♣ : 1♢, 2♠, but the final contract is reasonable.

You are the beneficiary of the ♣7 lead: eight – two . . .
What do you discard? Plan the play.

14. Teams: Dealer South : Both vulnerable

Contract: 6◇
Lead: ♣7

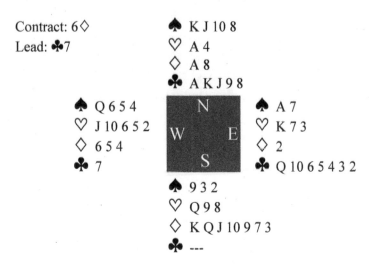

A heart lead would put paid to 6◇. If South ducks in dummy, the end is swift. If South plays ♡A to discard two hearts on the ♣A, ♣K, West ruffs and South later has to lose to the ♠A. On a spade lead, declarer will play low in dummy and succeed. On a trump lead, South will probably also fall back on the spade finesse.

After the ♣7 lead, declarer can win with the ♣A or ♣K, draw trumps and make 6◇ by playing for the ♠Q onside. Two hearts go on dummy's club winners. However, South played the ♣8 from dummy. East knew South had no clubs and that declarer could always set up an extra club trick later if East played the ♣10. East therefore gave South the extra club trick at once by playing low. This also muddied the waters as to the club position.

South discarded ♠2 on the ♣8. Assuming West had led ♣7 from ♣Q-10-7, South continued with ♣A, pitching ♠3. West ruffed and switched to ♡5. In desperation, South played low in dummy. East won and cashed the ♠A. South was two down.'

Every slam is 50%. You either make it or you don't.

15. Teams: Dealer East : North-South vulnerable

♠ 8 5 3
♡ K 5
♢ 8 7 5 3 2
♣ A 10 5

♠ K 4
♡ A 10 4
♢ K Q J 10 9 6 4
♣ 7

West	North	East	South
		Pass	1 ♢
3 ♣ (1)	3 ♢	Pass	5 ♢
Pass	Pass	Pass	

(1) 6+ clubs, 11-14 points

West leads the ♡8. Plan the play.

15. Teams: Dealer East : North-South vulnerable

Contract: 5♦
Lead: ♡8

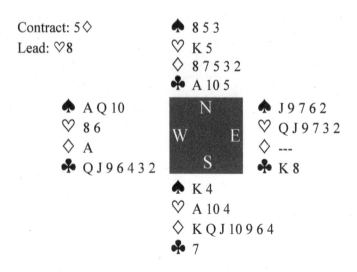

```
              ♠ 8 5 3
              ♡ K 5
              ♦ 8 7 5 3 2
              ♣ A 10 5

♠ A Q 10          N          ♠ J 9 7 6 2
♡ 8 6                        ♡ Q J 9 7 3 2
♦ A          W       E       ♦ ---
♣ Q J 9 6 4 3 2    S         ♣ K 8

              ♠ K 4
              ♡ A 10 4
              ♦ K Q J 10 9 6 4
              ♣ 7
```

Given West's 3♣ jump-overcall, showing the values for a
minimum opening hand, the ♠A is very likely to be with West.
You are in danger of losing a diamond and two spades. Your best
hope is that the ♦A is with West.

Take the ♡A, cross to the ♣A, ruff a club, cross to the ♡K and
ruff dummy's last club. Continue with your third heart. If West
were to follow to the third heart, you ruff in dummy and then exit
with a diamond. West wins but is endplayed. A club allows you to
ruff in dummy and discard a spade and playing a spade gives you
a trick with the ♠K.

When West shows out on the third heart, West has a choice of
poisons. If West discards, ruff the heart and play a diamond. If
West ruffs the third heart, West is endplayed for the same effect.
West could have avoided the endplay by leading the ♦A.

*A gentleman is someone who never strikes his bridge partner
without provocation.*

16. Teams: Dealer East : North-South vulnerable

♠ 10 7 5
♡ K 10 9 2
♢ 10 8
♣ 8 7 3 2

♠ A K Q J 8 4
♡ A J 3
♢ K 7 4 2
♣ ---

West	North	East	South
		Pass	1♠
2♣	Pass	3♣	Double (1)
Pass	4♠	All pass	

(1) For takeout

West leads the ♣K. Plan the play.

16. Teams: Dealer East : North-South vulnerable

Contract: 4♠
Lead: ♣K

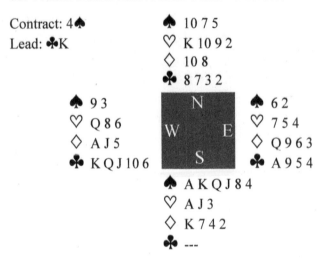

♠ 10 7 5
♡ K 10 9 2
♢ 10 8
♣ 8 7 3 2

♠ 9 3
♡ Q 8 6
♢ A J 5
♣ K Q J 10 6

♠ 6 2
♡ 7 5 4
♢ Q 9 6 3
♣ A 9 5 4

♠ A K Q J 8 4
♡ A J 3
♢ K 7 4 2
♣ ---

You need to ruff at least one diamond in dummy and so you ruff
the club and lead a low diamond. West wins with the ♢J and
plays a spade. You win in hand and play another low diamond:
five – ten – queen and East returns a spade. You win and play
another low diamond, ace, ruffed. With the ♢K high, you now
have ten tricks. If you pick up the ♡Q, you make an overtrick.

After ruffing the ♣K lead, it is important not to play a round of
trumps before leading a low diamond (such as a spade to the ten
and a diamond to the king). With the trumps 2-2, that does not
cost you here, but if the trumps were 3-1, they could eliminate
dummy's trumps before you can score a diamond ruff. If you do
not score a ruff in dummy and mispick the hearts, you would be
one down.

Playing a low diamond at trick 2 does not guarantee the contract,
but it does ensure at least one diamond ruff. After that, chances for
success are very strong.

Gross blunder: Partner's 144th mistake of the session.

17. Teams: Dealer South : Both vulnerable

```
              ♠ 9 6 5
              ♡ 9
              ♢ K Q J 10 5
              ♣ K J 9 4
```

```
              ♠ A K 4
              ♡ A K
              ♢ 8 7 6 3 2
              ♣ A 6 5
```

West	North	East	South
			1♢
Pass	2♢ (1)	Pass	4♢ (2)
Pass	4♠ (3)	Pass	4NT (4)
Pass	5♢ (5)	Pass	6♢
Pass	Pass	Pass	

(1) Inverted raise, 4+ diamonds, 10+ points, forcing
(2) Asking for key cards for diamonds
(3) One key card
(4) Asking for the trump queen
(5) 'I have the trump queen.'

West leads the ♡Q. Plan the play.

17. Teams: Dealer South : Both vulnerable

Contract: 6◇
Lead: ♡Q

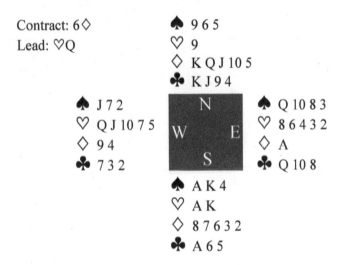

The simple line is to win ♡A, knock out the ◇A and then hope to avoid a club loser. As you can see, this line would fail.

A much better line, with only slight risk is to take the ♡A, ♡K (discarding a spade from dummy), followed by ♠A, ♠K and a third spade, ruffed high in dummy. The risk is that someone ruffs the second heart or the first or second spade (not likely), but if you have survived thus far, now is the time to lead a trump.

East wins, but with no diamond as a safe exit, East has to play a major, giving you a ruff-and-discard or play a club, eliminating any problem there.

If West happened to have the ◇A bare, then on the layout above, a club exit would defeat you, but if West had ♣10-x-x and East ♣Q-x-x, then when West exits with a low club, dummy's ♣9 will force out the ♣Q. If East covers the ♣9 with the ♣10, you win and then finesse the ♣J, hoping West has the ♣Q.

Cover an honour with an honour: A pyramid scheme for judges.

18. Pairs: Dealer South : Both vulnerable

♠ 9 8 6
♥ A Q 6
♦ J 9 6 3
♣ K 5 2

♠ A K Q 5 3
♥ K 9 8 5 3
♦ 10
♣ A 8

West	North	East	South
			1♠
Pass	2♠	Pass	4♠
Pass	Pass	Pass	

West leads the ♣J. Plan the play. Trumps will turn out to be 3-2. Remember, you are playing Pairs.

18. Pairs: Dealer South : Both vulnerable

Contract: 4♠
Lead: ♣J

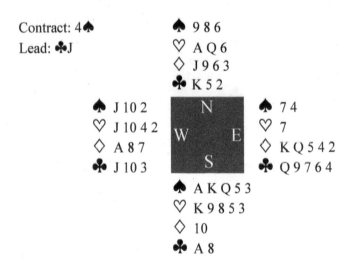

```
                    ♠ 9 8 6
                    ♡ A Q 6
                    ◇ J 9 6 3
                    ♣ K 5 2
    ♠ J 10 2          N          ♠ 7 4
    ♡ J 10 4 2    W       E      ♡ 7
    ◇ A 8 7                      ◇ K Q 5 4 2
    ♣ J 10 3          S          ♣ Q 9 7 6 4
                    ♠ A K Q 5 3
                    ♡ K 9 8 5 3
                    ◇ 10
                    ♣ A 8
```

At pairs, it may not be enough to make your game if others are making an overtrick or two. On the actual layout, you can make eleven tricks routinely: win the club lead, draw trumps and set up the hearts. You have only two losers, but also only eleven tricks.

In a good field, +650 should be a bottom score or perhaps a shared bottom, as there is a comfortable path to twelve tricks. Win the ♣J lead with the ♣K and play ♠A, ♠K. When all follow, continue with ♡A, ♡Q. If all follow, draw the last trump and claim twelve tricks. When East discards on the second heart, cross to ♡K and ruff a heart. Return to the ♣A and draw the last trump for +680.

If West began with three trumps and a singleton heart, it would not matter that West ruffed the ♡Q. On regaining the lead, you cash the ♡K and ruff a heart for eleven tricks, the same result as if you had drawn the last trump.

Surprisingly, of 21 declarers in 4♠, only ten made twelve tricks.

Concentration: Ever present on the irrelevant hands and never present on the critical ones.

19. Teams: Dealer South : Both vulnerable

```
              ♠ K 7 5 3 2
              ♡ Q 5
              ◇ 10
              ♣ A K J 9 4
                  N
              W       E
                  S
              ♠ A 6
              ♡ J 3 2
              ◇ K Q J 9 7
              ♣ Q 6 2
```

West	North	East	South
			1◇
Pass	1♠	Pass	1NT (1)
Pass	3♣ (2)	Pass	3◇ (3)
Pass	3♡ (4)	Pass	3NT
Pass	Pass	Pass	

(1) Minimum opening
(2) Game-force, at least 5-5 in spades and clubs
(3) Strength in diamonds
(4) 'I have some help in hearts.'

West leads the ♡A: five – ten (encouraging) – two, followed by the ♡K: queen – four – three and the ♡7: ♠2 – ♡8 – ♡J.
Plan the play.

19. Teams: Dealer South : Both vulnerable

Contract: 3NT
Lead: ♡A

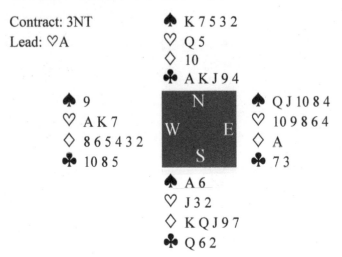

♠ K 7 5 3 2
♡ Q 5
♢ 10
♣ A K J 9 4

♠ 9
♡ A K 7
♢ 8 6 5 4 3 2
♣ 10 8 5

♠ Q J 10 8 4
♡ 10 9 8 6 4
♢ A
♣ 7 3

♠ A 6
♡ J 3 2
♢ K Q J 9 7
♣ Q 6 2

After ♡A, ♡K and a third heart, you can place West with five hearts and the ♢A (hardly possible with West passing) or, more likely, East began with five hearts. East did encourage hearts and West might have led a low heart initially with A-K to five hearts.

You could try a low diamond from hand or cross to dummy with a club and lead a low diamond, hoping East has the ♢A and plays second-hand low. This will not work in real life. Either player with ♢A and two winning hearts will grab the ♢A and cash them. Also, the actual layout precludes East playing second-hand-low.

A genuine hope is that the hand with the ♢A has no more hearts, but if so, there is no rush to play diamonds. You might as well cash the clubs first. As the cards lie, East is in trouble on the run of the clubs. With one club to go, East has ♠Q-J-10, ♡9-6, ♢A. What can East discard on the last club? Not the ♢A. Another spade gives South four spade tricks and so East discards a heart. Now you can afford to play a diamond and make nine tricks. You succeed even if East's hand pattern is 4-5-1-3 with the ♢A.

Bridge players and romantics love squeezes.

20. Teams: Dealer North : Nil vulnerable

♠ Q 10 8 7 3
♡ A 9 5
◇ 9
♣ K 8 5 2

♠ J 9 4
♡ K 3 2
◇ A J 8 6 5
♣ A Q

West	North	East	South
	Pass	Pass	1NT (1)
Pass	2♡ (2)	Pass	2♠
Pass	2NT (3)	Pass	4♠
Pass	Pass	Pass	

(1) 15-17 points
(2) Transfer to spades
(3) Inviting game

West leads the ♡7. Plan the play.

20. Teams: Dealer North : Nil vulnerable

Contract: 4♠
Lead: ♡7

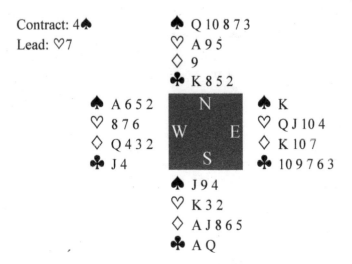

♠ Q 10 8 7 3
♡ A 9 5
♢ 9
♣ K 8 5 2

♠ A 6 5 2
♡ 8 7 6
♢ Q 4 3 2
♣ J 4

♠ K
♡ Q J 10 4
♢ K 10 7
♣ 10 9 7 6 3

♠ J 9 4
♡ K 3 2
♢ A J 8 6 5
♣ A Q

In a National Open Teams, several declarers chose this losing line: Win ♡K, cash ♣A, ♣Q, ♡2 to ♡A, ♣K and discard ♡3. West ruffed the ♣K and now could defeat 4♠ by playing a low spade. East wins and plays another club. South ruffs, West over-ruffs and now another spade from West leaves dummy with a heart loser.

Had the ♣K survived, South could make 11 tricks by ruffing the heart loser, ♢A, diamond ruff and club ruff, thus losing only the top spades. However, at 30%, a 5-2 club break is not that remote.

You can afford to lose two spades and a heart. Ruffing dummy's club loser is vital. Win trick 1 with ♡K, cash ♣A, ♣Q, ♢A, diamond ruff with ♠3 and play dummy's low club, ruffing with ♠9. If that wins, cross to ♡A and ruff ♣K with ♠J. Ten tricks.

If West over-ruffs the ♠9 and the defence can then play two more rounds of trumps, you are fine. If West over-ruffs ♠9 and plays ♠2 to East's ♠K and East plays another club, ruff with the ♠J.

Bridge cynic: One who places all of partner's actions into two classes: patently bad and probably bad.

21. Teams: Dealer South : East-West vulnerable

♠ J 7 5
♡ A 7
♢ A Q J 8 7
♣ J 9 2

♠ Q 9 8 4 2
♡ J 9 5
♢ K 10
♣ A K 8

West	North	East	South
			1♠
Pass	2♢	3♡ (1)	Pass
Pass	4♠	Pass	Pass
Double	Pass	Pass	Pass

(1) Weak jump-overcall

West leads the ♡2. Plan the play.

21. Teams: Dealer South : East-West vulnerable

Contract: 4♠
Lead: ♡2

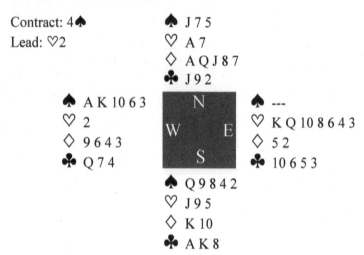

```
                    ♠ J 7 5
                    ♡ A 7
                    ◇ A Q J 8 7
                    ♣ J 9 2
♠ A K 10 6 3              N              ♠ ---
♡ 2                 W         E          ♡ K Q 10 8 6 4 3
◇ 9 6 4 3                S               ◇ 5 2
♣ Q 7 4                                  ♣ 10 6 5 3
                    ♠ Q 9 8 4 2
                    ♡ J 9 5
                    ◇ K 10
                    ♣ A K 8
```

West's double indicates at least four strong trumps and probably five. The ♡2 lead figures to be a singleton. Therefore, rise with the ♡A and start on the diamonds: ◇K, ◇10 to the ◇A and the ◇Q. When East fails to ruff this, the spade position is confirmed. You discard a heart on the ◇Q and another heart on the ◇J.

Continue with the fifth diamond and pitch the ♣8. West ruffs, but has no good move. You win the club exit and play the ♠8 or ♠9. If West ducks, you duck in dummy. If West takes with a top trump and returns a club, you win and lead another low spade. No matter how West plays, you lose just three trump tricks.

There are three key elements to ensure winning at bridge:
1. Tell no one else the key elements.
2.
3.

22. Teams: Dealer South : East-West vulnerable

♠ J 9 8 2
♡ J 8 7
♢ 9 4
♣ A J 10 6

♠ A K Q 7 6 4
♡ 9 5 4
♢ 3
♣ K Q 9

West	North	East	South
			1♠
2♡	2♠	Double (1)	4♠
5♢	Pass	Pass	5♠
Pass	Pass	Pass	

(1) For takeout, shows both minors

West leads the ♣5. Plan the play.

22. Teams: Dealer South : East-West vulnerable

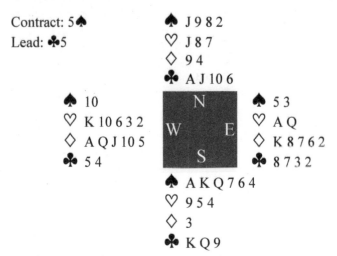

Contract: 5♠   ♠ J 9 8 2
Lead: ♣5   ♡ J 8 7
                      ◇ 9 4
                      ♣ A J 10 6

♠ 10   ♠ 5 3
♡ K 10 6 3 2   ♡ A Q
◇ A Q J 10 5   ◇ K 8 7 6 2
♣ 5 4   ♣ 8 7 3 2

                      ♠ A K Q 7 6 4
                      ♡ 9 5 4
                      ◇ 3
                      ♣ K Q 9

Against 5◇, the defence can take one spade and two clubs, but
there is scope for error. If North leads a spade, South wins and
must switch to clubs and not play a second spade. South was not
prepared to risk East-West making 5◇ and pushed on to 5♠.

A red-suit lead can take 5♠ two off, but West considered that too
risky. The ♣5 lead gives South a chance. As West did not lead a
heart, West does not have ♡A-K or ♡K-Q. If East has a bare top
heart or two honours doubleton, 5♠ can make if trumps are 2-1.

Win ♣K and play ♠A, ♠K. Continue with the ♣Q, ♣A and ♣J,
discarding your singleton diamond. Ruff a diamond, play a low
spade to dummy and ruff dummy's last diamond. You now have a
void in the minors in each hand. Exit with a low heart, ducking in
dummy. If East has ♡A, K, Q bare or ♡A-K, A-Q or K-Q, the
defence cannot cash three hearts. Either they set up the ♡J or give
you a ruff-and-discard and you lose only two hearts. Peter Lund of
Denmark did that in the 2002 European Open Teams to make 5♠.

If at first you don't succeed, you are just the same as 99.9% of all
bridge players.

23. Teams: Dealer West : East-West vulnerable

♠ Q 9 4
♡ 2
♢ K 8 6 4
♣ A 9 6 4 2

♠ A K 7 5 3 2
♡ ---
♢ A Q 9 5
♣ 10 5 3

West	North	East	South
1♡	Double (1)	4♡	6♠
Pass	Pass	Pass	

(1) Not recommended

West leads the ♢10. Plan the play.

23. Teams: Dealer West : East-West vulnerable

Contract: 6♠
Lead: ◇10

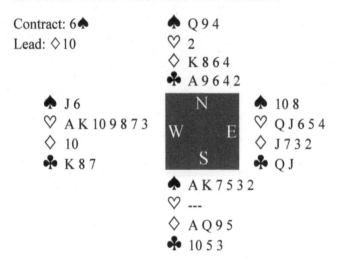

♠ Q 9 4
♡ 2
◇ K 8 6 4
♣ A 9 6 4 2

♠ J 6
♡ A K 10 9 8 7 3
◇ 10
♣ K 8 7

♠ 10 8
♡ Q J 6 5 4
◇ J 7 3 2
♣ Q J

♠ A K 7 5 3 2
♡ ---
◇ A Q 9 5
♣ 10 5 3

You need to deal with the two losers in clubs via an opposition error or via an endplay. For the endplay to operate, you will need spades to be 2-2 and you need to ruff dummy's ♡2. The ◇10 lead, probably a singleton, marks East with the ◇J.

Sartaj Hans of Australia made 6♠ this way. He took the ◇10 with the ◇A and played ♣10 at once. He was hoping West might cover the ♣10 with an honour from K-Q-x-x, K-J-x-x or Q-J-x-x.

When West played low on the ♣10, South rose with the ♣A, played ♣4 to ♣A and ♣2 to ♣Q and ruffed the ♡2. Then came ◇5 to ◇K and a finesse of the ◇9. He cashed the ◇Q and had a void in both hands in the red suits. He then exited with a club.

No matter what the defence did, declarer was home. If West rose with the ♣K, dummy's ♣9 would be high. When West ducked, East won but East had only hearts left. East had to give declarer a ruff-and-discard and away went South's third club.

Bridge does not have a 'happily ever after', but happy endings do still occur.

24. Teams: Dealer East : North-South vulnerable

♠ Q 7 6 2
♡ K 9 6 5
♢ A 4
♣ Q 9 2

♠ A 10 5 4
♡ Q 8 7 4 2
♢ K 8
♣ A J

West	North	East	South
		Pass	1♡
Pass	3♢ (1)	Pass	4♡
Pass	Pass	Pass	

(1) Bergen raise, 10-12 points, 4+ hearts

West leads the ♠8: two – jack – ace. Plan the play.

24. From the final of a National Open Teams, 2011

Contract: 4♡
Lead: ♠8

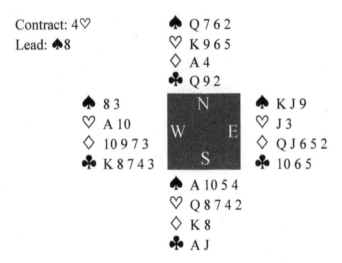

```
                    ♠ Q 7 6 2
                    ♡ K 9 6 5
                    ◇ A 4
                    ♣ Q 9 2
  ♠ 8 3                            ♠ K J 9
  ♡ A 10              N            ♡ J 3
  ◇ 10 9 7 3      W       E        ◇ Q J 6 5 2
  ♣ K 8 7 4 3         S            ♣ 10 6 5
                    ♠ A 10 5 4
                    ♡ Q 8 7 4 2
                    ◇ K 8
                    ♣ A J
```

The ♠8 could be a singleton, top from a doubleton, middle from 9-8-3 or even bottom from K-9-8. In any case, you have a spade loser and certainly might suffer a spade ruff. You have to lose a trump trick and if West has the ♣K, that could be a fourth loser.

Many declarers would simply play a trump at trick 2 and hope for the best. Now the defence can prevail. West takes ♡A at once and continues with ♠3. East wins and returns a spade. West ruffs and exits with a diamond. With the ♣K offside, you are one down.

A simple precaution can save you. You have two diamond winners and no more. It cannot hurt to cash them before playing a trump. After ◇A, ◇K and a trump, West can take the ♡A, play the ♠3 to the ♠K and receive a spade ruff. However, West is now down to diamonds and clubs only. A club return eliminates the club loser. So does a diamond. You ruff it in dummy and discard your ♣J.

If you fail to exercise precaution, there may be no cure.

25. Teams: Dealer South : Nil vulnerable

♠ A K J
♡ A K Q 5 3
♢ 9 8 7
♣ K 2

♠ Q 8 7
♡ 7 4
♢ A K
♣ A 10 8 7 6 4

West	North	East	South
			1♣
Pass	1♡	Pass	2♣
Pass	2♠ (1)	Pass	2NT (2)
Pass	6NT	All pass	

(1) South's 2♣ denied four spades and so North's 2♠ can be just showing a spade stopper.
(2) Promises a diamond stopper.

West leads the ♢Q. Plan the play.

25. Teams: Dealer South : Nil vulnerable

Contract: 6NT
Lead: ◇Q

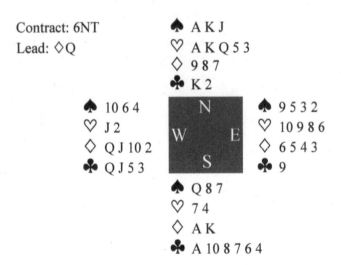

♠ A K J
♡ A K Q 5 3
◇ 9 8 7
♣ K 2

♠ 10 6 4
♡ J 2
◇ Q J 10 2
♣ Q J 5 3

♠ 9 5 3 2
♡ 10 9 8 6
◇ 6 5 4 3
♣ 9

♠ Q 8 7
♡ 7 4
◇ A K
♣ A 10 8 7 6 4

You have ten tricks on top. Two more could come from a 3-3 heart split, but that is a bit below a 36% chance. The clubs offer much better odds. The 3-2 split is about a 68% chance. How should you play the clubs? There will be no problem if they divide 3-2. Can you cater for any 4-1 breaks?

If East has Q-J-5-3, Q-9-5-3 or J-9-5-3, a low club will work. When West plays the Q, J or 9, dummy's king wins and you can then finesse against East on the next club, or if East plays high, you take the ♣A and knock out East's remaining high club. If the clubs do not behave, you can fall back on a 3-3 heart break.

That play will not work as the cards lie. A better move will. Play ♣10 at trick 2. Let it run if West plays low. All is well if clubs are 3-2. If West plays Q, J or 9, take ♣K and finesse against East on the way back. On the layout above, the ♣10 pins the ♣9 and you have twelve tricks whether West plays low on the ♣10 or covers.

Chance happens to us all, but to turn chance to account is the gift of the few. (Bluwer-Lytton)

26. Teams: Dealer South : Both vulnerable

♠ A K 10
♡ K 10 7 6
♢ A Q 10
♣ A K 6

♠ Q 9 7
♡ A J 8 3
♢ 9 8 4
♣ J 9 3

West	North	East	South
			Pass
Pass	1♣ (1)	Pass	1NT (2)
Pass	2♣ (3)	Pass	2♡ (4)
Pass	6♡	All pass	

(1) Artificial, 16+ points
(2) Balanced hand, 8-10 points
(3) Asking for 4-card majors
(4) Four hearts

West leads the ♠4. Plan the play.

26. Teams: Dealer South : Both vulnerable

Contract: 6♡   ♠ A K 10
Lead: ♠4   ♡ K 10 7 6
                    ◊ A Q 10
                    ♣ A K 6

```
        N
   W         E
        S
```

                  ♠ Q 9 7
                  ♡ A J 8 3
                  ◊ 9 8 4
                  ♣ J 9 3

North-South should adopt better bidding methods, such as 2NT over 2♣ to show some minimum 4-3-3-3 and 3NT as a 4-3-3-3 with maximum strength. Opener can still ask for a 4-card major.

This is an awful slam. You probably have a club loser. You have to find the ♡Q and even then you have to hope West has the ◊K and ◊J. Well, no use wishing you were only in game. Win trick 1 with the ♠A and pray that the cards lie well for you.

It is a pure guess where the ♡Q lies, but you can deal with a 4-1 trump break: ♡K and the ♡10 next or ♡A and the ♡J next. Since you will need entries to your hand for the diamond finesses, it is better to start with the ♡K. All follow. When you play the ♡10 next, East produces the ♡Q. You win and West follows.

The ♡J draws the missing trump and you finesse ◊10. It wins. You cross to ♠Q and finesse ◊Q. It wins. When you play ♣A, ♣K, the ♣Q falls. Making thirteen tricks will not dampen your partner's enthusiasm. West: ♠J 8 6 4 2 ♡5 4 2 ◊K J 7 ♣Q 4.

The future: When our partners do the right thing, our doubles for penalties are justified and our overbidding pays off for us.

27. Teams: Dealer North : Both vulnerable

♠ A 2
♡ A Q 10 9 3
♢ A K
♣ J 10 9 6

♠ Q J 8 7 5 3
♡ 8 6
♢ Q 6 5
♣ 5 3

West	North	East	South
	1♡	Pass	1♠
Pass	2♣	Pass	2♠
Pass	4♠	All pass	

West leads the ♣K and East encourages. West continues with the ♣Q and the ♣8: ten – ace – ♠3. Plan the play.

27. Teams: Dealer North : Both vulnerable

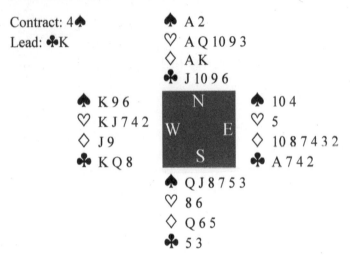

Contract: 4♠
Lead: ♣K

North:
♠ A 2
♥ A Q 10 9 3
♦ A K
♣ J 10 9 6

West:
♠ K 9 6
♥ K J 7 4 2
♦ J 9
♣ K Q 8

East:
♠ 10 4
♥ 5
♦ 10 8 7 4 3 2
♣ A 7 4 2

South:
♠ Q J 8 7 5 3
♥ 8 6
♦ Q 6 5
♣ 5 3

After ♣K, ♣Q and ♣8 to the ♣A, ruffed, South's problem is how to handle trumps. Even though the spade finesse works as the cards lie, that line is not best. It would fail if East wins with ♠K and returns the fourth club. Swap the East-West trumps to see what happens if you run ♠Q to East's ♠K and a club comes back.

Best is a low spade to the ♠A. That works if East has the ♠K bare. After the ♠A, cash ◊A, ◊K and only then play a second spade. If East wins the ♠K and plays a club, discard a heart and hope that East has the third spade or ruff the club high, draw the last trump and finesse the ♥Q. If West wins the second spade and plays a heart, you have to decide whether to finesse the ♥Q or take the ♥A and play the ♣J, hoping the player with the third spade also has the fourth club. The odds favour the ♥Q finesse.

Some played a low spade to ♠A and ♠2 at once. West took the ♠Q and exited with ◊9. Now declarer was doomed, as West's ♠9 would score a trick when declarer played ♣J from dummy.

The main lesson of history is the triumph of evil. The main lesson of bridge is the triumph of good.

28. Teams: Dealer South : Both vulnerable

♠ A 8 2
♡ K 9 5
◇ J 7 2
♣ Q J 10 4

♠ Q J 5
♡ A 10 6 2
◇ K Q 10 3
♣ K 8

West	North	East	South
			1NT
Pass	3NT	All pass	

West leads the ♠4, low from dummy, and East plays the ♠9. Plan the play.

28. Teams: Dealer South : Both vulnerable

Contract: 3NT
Lead: ♣4

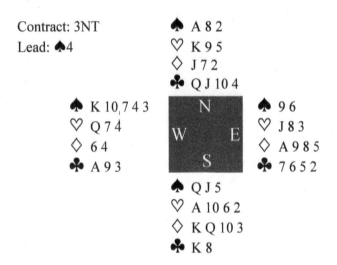

♠ A 8 2
♥ K 9 5
◊ J 7 2
♣ Q J 10 4

♠ K 10 7 4 3
♥ Q 7 4
◊ 6 4
♣ A 9 3

♠ 9 6
♥ J 8 3
◊ A 9 8 5
♣ 7 6 5 2

♠ Q J 5
♥ A 10 6 2
◊ K Q 10 3
♣ K 8

With four winners in the majors, you need five tricks from the minors. If you win and play on clubs first, you succeed. If you win and play diamonds first, you fail. East wins and returns a spade. Now West's spades will set up and West can cash the spade winners on winning the ♣A. You lose three spades and two aces.

Does that mean you should win and play a club at trick 2? That fails if East had the ♣A and West the ◊A. Picking the 'right' minor is a matter of luck. You are safe if spades are 4-3 or if West has five spades and East has both minor suit aces. One case where your play is critical is when West has five spades and the minor suit aces are split. From East's play of the ♠9 at trick 1, you can deduce that West has the ♠K. The right move is to duck the ♠9.

You still make two spade tricks, but now, after a spade return at trick 2, East has no spade to return when in with the ♣A or ◊A. Ducking at trick 1 will cost only if West has five spades and both minor aces.

In bridge, skill is the forerunner of good luck.

29. Teams: Dealer North : Both vulnerable

```
                    ♠ 7 6 3 2
                    ♡ A 5 4
                    ◇ A 3
                    ♣ A Q 10 5
                  ┌─────────┐
                  │    N    │
                  │ W     E │
                  │    S    │
                  └─────────┘
                    ♠ A K 5 4
                    ♡ Q J 6 3 2
                    ◇ 9 5
                    ♣ 6 2
```

West	North	East	South
	1♣	Pass	1♡
Pass	2♡	Pass	2♠
Pass	3♠	Pass	4♠
Pass	Pass	Pass	

West leads the ◇4. Plan the play.

How would you plan the play if West leads the ♣4?

29. Teams: Dealer North : Both vulnerable

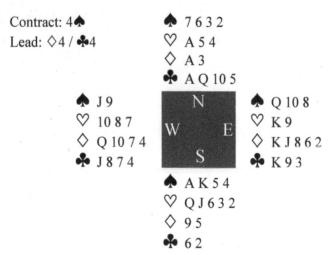

Contract: 4♠
Lead: ◇4 / ♣4

```
              ♠ 7 6 3 2
              ♡ A 5 4
              ◇ A 3
              ♣ A Q 10 5
  ♠ J 9                        ♠ Q 10 8
  ♡ 10 8 7          N          ♡ K 9
  ◇ Q 10 7 4    W     E        ◇ K J 8 6 2
  ♣ J 8 7 4         S          ♣ K 9 3
              ♠ A K 5 4
              ♡ Q J 6 3 2
              ◇ 9 5
              ♣ 6 2
```

You will lose a diamond and a heart. Assume spades are 3-2. If they are 4-1, you have no chance. You could lose a club if West comes in again and switches to a club. To reduce that risk, duck the ◇4 lead. East wins and will probably return a diamond. Now play ♠A, ♠K, ♡A and ♡4. East wins and can cash the ♠Q, but is endplayed, either giving you a ruff-and-discard to pitch a club or leading into the ♣A-Q. If West had won the second heart and switched to a club, you would finesse the ♣Q as your best chance.

Note that it would be poor to take ◇A, ♠A, ♠K and lead the ♡Q for a finesse. That costs not only if there is a singleton ♡K about, but also on the actual deal. East wins the ♡K, cashes ◇K and ♠Q and exits with ♡9. Now you need the club finesse and 4♠ fails.

On the ♣4 lead, play the ♣10. When that forces out the ♣K, you have a discard for your diamond loser. If East wins with the ♣J and switches to a diamond, take the ◇A, ♠A, ♠K and finesse the ♣Q as your best chance.

Success covers a multitude of blunders.

30. Teams: Dealer North : Both vulnerable

```
            ♠ 8 3
            ♡ K 10 9 5 4 3
            ◇ K 8
            ♣ 9 8 7

            ♠ A Q 7
            ♡ Q 8 6 2
            ◇ A 7 3
            ♣ K Q 3
```

West	North	East	South
	Pass	Pass	1NT (1)
Pass	2◇ (2)	Pass	3♡ (3)
Pass	4♡	All pass	

(1) 15-17 points
(2) Transfer to hearts
(3) Maximum 1NT with 4-5 hearts

West leads the ♣6: seven – ten – king. Plan the play.

30. Teams: Dealer North : Both vulnerable

Contract: 4♡
Lead: ♣6

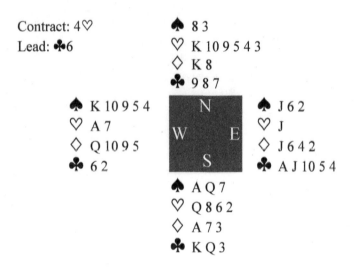

♠ 8 3
♡ K 10 9 5 4 3
◇ K 8
♣ 9 8 7

♠ K 10 9 5 4
♡ A 7
◇ Q 10 9 5
♣ 6 2

♠ J 6 2
♡ J
◇ J 6 4 2
♣ A J 10 5 4

♠ A Q 7
♡ Q 8 6 2
◇ A 7 3
♣ K Q 3

East did well to duck the first club. If East takes ♣A and returns a club, South wins and can play a heart to make ten tricks easily.

Many Souths would be tempted to play a trump at trick 2, but that road leads to perdition. West takes the ♡A and reverts to the ♣2. East wins and gives West a club ruff. When West exits with a diamond, South loses a spade later for one down.

Tina Zines of Australia spotted the danger of the club ruff. Why else would East duck the first club? Before touching trumps, she eliminated the diamonds: ◇K, ◇A and a diamond ruff. Then came a trump the queen and ace. West continued with the ♣2. East took the ♣A and gave West a club ruff. West was down to spades and the ◇Q. A spade would eliminate the spade loser. The ◇Q would allow South to pitch a spade from dummy and ruff in hand. Either way, South had ten tricks.

Reality refuses to go away even if you stop believing in it.

31. Teams: Dealer South : East-West vulnerable

	♠ K 8
	♡ Q 10 8
	◇ A J 8 7 3
	♣ 5 4 2

	♠ A Q 9 7 6
	♡ K 7 6 5 3
	◇ Q 6
	♣ K

West	North	East	South
			1♠
2♣	2◇	Pass	2♡
Pass	2♠	Pass	3♡
Pass	4♡	All pass	

West leads the ♣A, followed by the ♣Q, which you ruff. You play the ♡5: nine – ten – two, followed by the ♠K and the ♠8 to the ♠A, all following. What next?

31. Teams: Dealer South : East-West vulnerable

Contract: 4 ♡
Lead: ♣A

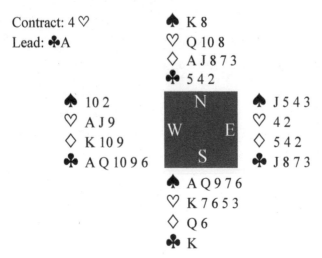

          ♠ K 8
          ♡ Q 10 8
          ◇ A J 8 7 3
          ♣ 5 4 2

♠ 10 2   ♠ J 5 4 3
♡ A J 9   N   ♡ 4 2
◇ K 10 9   W   E   ◇ 5 4 2
♣ A Q 10 9 6   S   ♣ J 8 7 3

          ♠ A Q 9 7 6
          ♡ K 7 6 5 3
          ◇ Q 6
          ♣ K

After ruffing the second club, South played ♡5 to the ♡10 and
the ♠K, followed by ♠8 to the ♠A. The simplest continuation is
to ruff a low spade in dummy and play the ♡Q. If West switches
to a diamond, take the ◇A, ruff a club, draw the last trump and
claim. You have four spades, a spade ruff, four hearts and the ◇A.

As the cards lie, you can finesse ◇J, cash ◇A, ruff a diamond and
lead the ♠Q. Nothing West can do can harm you. If West ruffs
with ♡J, you over-ruff with ♡Q, ruff a club and lead another
spade to score the ♡8, *en passant*. This line brings in 11 tricks.

In a national teams declarer finessed ◇J and then played the ♡Q.
West won and continued clubs. South ruffed. Down to ♠Q-9-7,
♡K, ◇Q opposite ♡8, ◇A-8-7-3, South needed to play ◇Q to
the ◇A, ruff a diamond and lead a spade to score the ♡8. Instead,
South played the ♠Q. West ruffed with the ♡J and played another
club. No matter where South ruffed that, he could not avoid losing
another trick to go one down in a simple and stone-cold contract.

Half of this game is 90% logic.

32. Teams: Dealer South : East-West vulnerable

♠ 7 6 2
♡ J
♢ J 10 6 3
♣ 10 9 5 3 2

♠ A Q J 10 4
♡ K 6 2
♢ A
♣ A Q 8 6

West	North	East	South
			1♠
Pass	3♠ (1)	Double (2)	4♠
Pass	Pass	Pass	
(1) Weaker than 2♠			
(2) For takeout			

West leads the ♡10: jack – ace – two. East returns the ♡4: six – three – ♠2. You play the ♣2: four – queen – seven. How should you continue?

32. Teams: Dealer South : East-West vulnerable

Contract: 4♠
Lead: ♡10

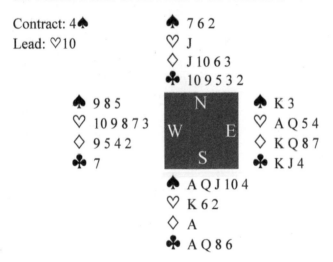

Many would lead the ♣7 from West, but that would not beat 4♠. South would capture East's card and play ♠A, ♠Q. East wins and can give West a club ruff, but at the cost of allowing you to set up the clubs. The only other trick for the defence would be the ♡A.

After the actual lead of the ♡10: jack – ace – two and the return of the ♡4: six – three – ♠2, South played the ♣2: four – queen – seven and continued with the ♠A and ♠10. That was fatal. East won and played the ♣K, ace, ruffed, and South still had to lose to the ♣J. One down.

After the ♣Q wins, South should ruff the ♡K and play the ♠7: three – queen – five. If the finesse loses, East has no quick entry to play a club for West to ruff. When the ♠Q wins, South plays the ♠A and draws the last trump. South continues with the ♣A and another club, making 11 tricks. If East began with ♠K-x-x, South loses a spade trick, but still makes ten tricks.

'State-of-the-match play': A phrase used in the post mortem to excuse your losing decisions.

33. Pairs: Dealer West : Nil vulnerable

<pre>
                    ♠ J 6
                    ♡ A 7 3
                    ◇ Q J 10 6 4
                    ♣ 9 8 3
                         N
                   W   E
                         S
                    ♠ Q 4
                    ♡ K J 10
                    ◇ 9 8 2
                    ♣ A K J 6 2
</pre>

West	North	East	South
1♠	Pass	2♠	3♣
Pass	Pass	Pass	

West leads the ◇A: four – seven . . . the opponents play high-encourage. Which diamond do you play?

West switches to the ♠10: six – ace – four and East returns the ♠2: queen – king – jack. West shifts to the ♡8: three – queen – king. How would you continue?

33. Pairs: Dealer West : Nil vulnerable

Contract: 3♣
Lead: ◇A

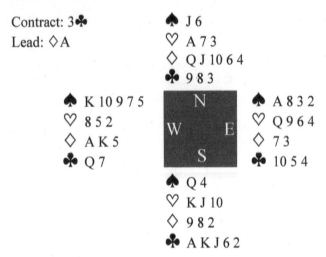

You must check the opponents' leading and signalling agreements at the start of each round. Sometimes it pays to play a high spot-card to try to mislead an opponent, but that is unwise here. If you play ◇8 or ◇9, West can tell that East's ◇7 is a singleton or top from a doubleton. Continue with ◇K and give East a ruff.

South should play the ◇2 at trick 1. West might now read East's ◇7 as the bottom from 9-8-7. Indeed, West switched to a spade to the ace and won the ♠2 return with the ♠K. West could have continued diamonds now, but shifted to the ♡8, hoping East had the ♡K. South captured the ♡Q and had to handle the clubs.

If you are to become a great bridge player, a requisite is to count. South counted the points revealed. North-South had 22 HCP, East-West 18. East had shown up with 6 HCP and so the ♣Q figured to be with West for the opening bid. South played ♣A, ♣K and was rewarded when the ♣Q dropped. South drew the last trump and made nine tricks for an excellent score.

25% of all bridge players understand counting and 85% do not.

34. Pairs: Dealer East : Both vulnerable

♠ Q 10
♡ A 9 3
◇ Q J 10
♣ Q 10 6 5 3

♠ K J 7 4
♡ Q 5 2
◇ A 6 5
♣ A J 9

West	North	East	South
		Pass	1NT (1)
Pass	3NT	All pass	

(1) 15-17 points

West leads the ♠6: queen – ace – four and East returns the ♠8:
seven – three – ten. South plays the ♣10: four – nine – two, the
♣3: eight – jack – seven, followed by the ♣A: ♠5 – ♣5 – ♣K.
You have ten tricks for sure, but you are playing Pairs.

How would you continue?

34. Pairs: Dealer East : Both vulnerable

Contract: 3NT
Lead: ♠6

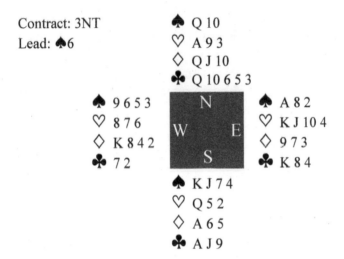

After the spade lead to the ace and the spade return, won by the
♠10, South took two club finesses, followed by the ♣A.

If you cross to ♡A and cash the clubs, you have no good discards.
If you pitch two diamonds and play a heart towards the queen, you
might not even make ten tricks. To pitch two hearts and take the
diamond finesse comes with equal risk.

Seeking overtricks, declarer tried a different tack. South crossed to
♡A and played the ◇Q. If it lost to the ◇K, the worst that could
happen was for West to play a heart, holding South to ten tricks. It
went ◇Q: three – five – two! Fooled, South continued with ◇J:
nine – six – king. When West returned ◇4, South won, but
dummy's clubs were marooned. After cashing ♠K, ♠J, South had
to lead away from the ♡Q and so made only nine tricks.

South should have been content to make eleven tricks. After the
♣A, play a low diamond. This ensures eleven tricks with no risk.

If you can win by playing safe, why take any risk?

35. Teams: Dealer South : Nil vulnerable

```
              ♠ 7 4 2
              ♡ A K Q 6
              ◇ Q 5 3
              ♣ Q 7 3

         N
     W       E
         S

              ♠ A K 8 6
              ♡ 5 4 2
              ◇ K
              ♣ A K J 5 4
```

West	North	East	South
			1♣
Pass	1♡	Pass	1♠ (1)
Pass	2◇ (2)	Pass	3♡ (3)
Pass	4♣ (4)	Pass	4◇ (5)
Pass	4♡ (5)	Pass	4♠ (5)
Pass	4NT	Pass	5♣ (6)
Pass	6♣	All pass	

(1) 5+ clubs, 4 spades (2) Fourth-suit, forcing to game
(3) Three hearts, better than a minimum opening
(4) Club support
(5) Cue-bid, first- or second-round control
(6) 0 or 3 key cards

West leads the ♠Q: two – three – ace. You play ♣A, ♣K and the
♣4 to the ♣Q. West discards the ♠9. After the ◇3: two – king –
ace, West returns the ♠J: four – five – king. Proceed.

35. Teams: Dealer South : Nil vulnerable

Contract: 6♣
Lead: ♠Q

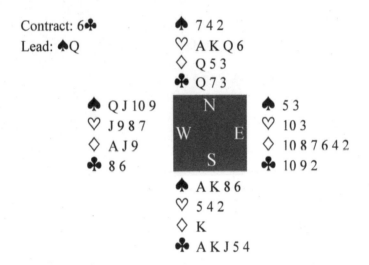

South wins the ♠Q lead and draws trumps, West pitching ♣9. After ◊3: two – king – ace, West returns ♠J: four – five – king.

You have eleven tricks. The twelfth must come from the hearts. If they split 3-3 initially, all is well, but a 4-2 split is more likely. There is no rush to test the hearts. If you play ♡A, ♡K, ♡Q next, you will fail when hearts do turn out to be 4-2.

Play a heart to the ace, cash the ◊Q, discarding ♣6, and ruff ◊5. West has ♠10, ♡J-9-8, South has ♠8, ♡5-4, ♣J and dummy has ♠7, ♡K-Q-6. Now play your last club, pitching dummy's ♠7. If West discards ♠10, your ♠8 is high. If West throws a heart, dummy's ♡6 becomes a winner. Your last club squeezed West.

It costs you nothing to play off the last club. If the hearts are 3-3 all along, they will still be 3-3 after the last club.

Squeeze: A play whereby the last card you hold has mysteriously become a winner, just as you were about to concede one off.

36. Teams: Dealer North : Both vulnerable

♠ A K 8 7 4
♡ K 10 2
♢ Q 10 2
♣ Q J

♠ 9 6
♡ A Q 7 5 4
♢ 7 4
♣ 8 5 4 2

West	North	East	South
	1♠	2♣	Pass
Pass	Double (1)	Pass	3♡
Pass	Pass	Pass	

(1) For takeout

As a bid of 2♡ would not promise any values, South jumped to 3♡ to show some strength in case North had a very strong hand. Some would have doubled 2♣ initially, as a negative double.

West leads the ♣6: queen – king – two. East continues with ♣A: four – ♠3 – ♣J and switches to the ♢A, followed by the ♢9 to West's ♢K. North plays a third diamond: queen – ♡6 – ♡7.

You continue with ♠A, ♠K, all following, and the ♠4: queen . . . How will you play from here?

36. Teams: Dealer North : Both vulnerable

Contract: 3♡
Lead: ♣6

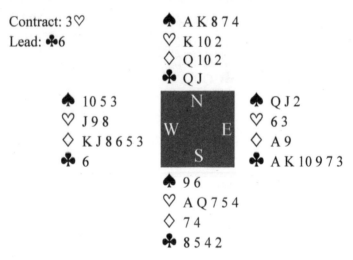

          ♠ A K 8 7 4
          ♡ K 10 2
          ◇ Q 10 2
          ♣ Q J

♠ 10 5 3   ♠ Q J 2
♡ J 9 8   ♡ 6 3
◇ K J 8 6 5 3   ◇ A 9
♣ 6   ♣ A K 10 9 7 3

          ♠ 9 6
          ♡ A Q 7 5 4
          ◇ 7 4
          ♣ 8 5 4 2

After ♣K and ♣A by East, West discarding ♠3, what do you
know? *Answer:* East began with six clubs.

After ◇A, ◇K, third diamond, ruffed by East, over-ruffed by you,
what do you know? *Answer:* East began with two diamonds.

After ♠A, ♠K and a third spade, to which East follows with the
♠Q, what do you know?
Answer: East began with three spades and hence a 3-2-2-6 pattern.

You have already lost four tricks. As West discarded a spade at
trick 2, you must ruff high on the ♠Q, else West over-ruffs. As
East ruffed once, East is down to one heart. After you ruff the ♠Q
with the ♡Q, cash the ♡A and finesse the ♡10. The finesse of the
♡10 is a sure thing. Cash the ♡K to draw West's last trump and
dummy's spades are high, making 3♡ for +140.

The beginning and end of good play is counting.

37. Teams: Dealer East : Nil vulnerable

♠ 8 4
♡ A Q 10
◇ K J 8 6 2
♣ A 9 7

♠ K Q J 7 6 5 2
♡ J 3
◇ A 10
♣ J 3

West	North	East	South
		3♡	3♠
Pass	3NT	Pass	4♠
Pass	Pass	Pass	

West leads the ♡2, clearly a singleton. You take the ♡A and play the ♠4: ♣5 (odd-card = encouraging) – ♠K – ♠A. West shifts to the ♣2. Plan the play.

37. Teams: Dealer East : Nil vulnerable

Contract: 4♠
Lead: ♡2

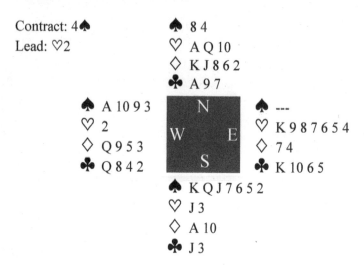

	♠ 8 4
	♡ A Q 10
	◇ K J 8 6 2
	♣ A 9 7

West:
♠ A 10 9 3
♡ 2
◇ Q 9 5 3
♣ Q 8 4 2

East:
♠ ---
♡ K 9 8 7 6 5 4
◇ 7 4
♣ K 10 6 5

South:
♠ K Q J 7 6 5 2
♡ J 3
◇ A 10
♣ J 3

After winning trick 1 with the ♡A, South played the ♠4, East
discarding the ♣5 (odd-encouraging). The ♠K lost to the ♠A and
West switched to the ♣2.

You are sure to have two spade losers and clearly you cannot
afford to duck the club. East would win and cash the ♡K for one
down. Your best hope is that the ◇Q is with West (or, less likely,
that East began with the ◇Q singleton).

Take the ♣A, play ♠Q, ♣J, ◇A and the ◇10, overtaking with
the ◇J when West plays low. When the ◇J wins, discard a loser
on the ◇K and you have ten tricks, +420.

*An optimist believes that his bridge partner is playing as well as
he possibly can. The pessimist fears that this is probably true.*

38. Teams: Dealer East : Both vulnerable

```
            ♠ A 8 7 3
            ♡ J 6
            ◇ A J 9 2
            ♣ K 8 2

            ♠ ---
            ♡ A 10 3
            ◇ K Q 8 3
            ♣ A Q J 10 9 3
```

West	North	East	South
		2♣ (1)	Double (2)
3♡ (3)	Double (4)	Pass	6♣
Pass	Pass	Pass	

(1) Weak, both majors
(2) Takeout
(3) Primarily pre-emptive
(4) Take-out, good hand

West leads the ◇4: two – ♣5 – ◇3. East switches to the ♡2. Plan the play.

38. Teams: Dealer East : Both vulnerable

Contract: 6♣
Lead: ◇4

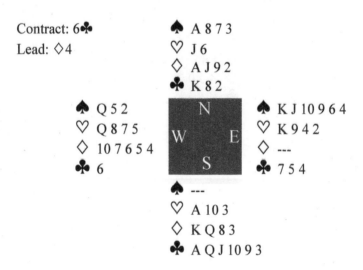

You naturally take East's ♡2 switch with the ♡A. You have no legitimate play for your slam. You can play a second heart and settle for one down, but that will be a terrible result if the opponents reach 6NT or play in 6♣ without a diamond lead or stop in game. If so, going two down will cost you at most 1 Imp.

After taking the ♡A, you could try some subterfuge by drawing trumps, playing diamonds ending in hand and then running the rest of the clubs. That leaves you with ♡10-3 and a possible two down, but if the opponents are not very strong in defence, maybe they will both decide to guard the spades and come down two spades each. They will then have discarded their hearts, each hoping the other is guarding hearts and your two hearts will be winners. It should not work, and against strong defenders it will not work, but it cannot hurt you to set them a trap.

You can fool some of the people all of the time. You should concentrate on those.

39. Teams: Dealer West : Nil vulnerable

♠ K 4 3
♡ K 9 5 3
♢ Q J 5
♣ A 9 2

♠ Q J 9 8 5 2
♡ 6 2
♢ K 6 3
♣ Q 8

West	North	East	South
Pass	1♣ (1)	Pass	1♠
Pass	1NT	Pass	2♠
Pass	Pass	Pass	

(1) Playing a 1NT opening as 15-17

1. West leads the ♡Q: three – four – six.
2. West switches to the ♣J: two – king – eight.
3. East returns the ♡10: two – ace – five.
4. West continues with the ♡8: nine – jack – ♠5.

Do you agree with South's play so far? How would you continue as South?

39. Teams: Dealer West : Nil vulnerable

Contract: 2♠
Lead: ♡Q

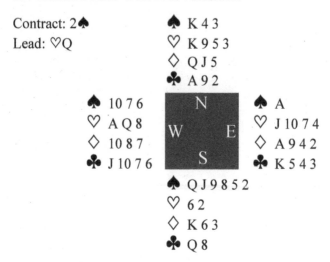

After the daring ♡Q lead (not recommended, although it worked), West shifted to the ♣J: two – king – eight. East returned ♡10: two – ace – five. West continued with ♡8: nine – jack – ♠5.

South played ♠J: six – three – ace. East cashed ◇A and returned the ♡7, ruffed with the ♠Q. When South played ♠9: seven – king – ♣3, he was one down, while most Souths made nine tricks.

South could have made 2♠ easily by playing the cost-free ♡K at trick 4. Even if East ruffs the ♡K with a low trump, South over-ruffs and makes eight tricks.

At trick 5, instead of ♠J from hand, how about ♣Q to ♣A and a low spade from dummy? The rest is easy when East plays the ♠A or if East plays low and South's ♠Q wins. Playing the first spade from dummy can cost only if East has ◇A and West ♠A-10-x. Then, after the ♠Q is taken by ♠A, a diamond to the ace and the ♡7 from East, South would have to misguess trumps to go off.

All bridge players should be buried with honours.

40. Pairs: Dealer South : North-South vulnerable

♠ Q J 7
♡ Q J 4 3
◇ K 8 3 2
♣ A 4

♠ A K 9 6 4
♡ A 8 7 5
◇ 6 5
♣ K 9

West	North	East	South
			1♠
Pass	2◇	Pass	2♡
Pass	3♡	Pass	3♠ (1)
Pass	4♣ (1)	Pass	4♡ (2)
Pass	Pass	Pass	

(1) Cue-bid, first- or second-round control
(2) Denying diamond control

West leads the ◇Q: two – four – five and continues with the ◇J: three – ace – six. East shifts to the ♣3. Plan the play.

40. Pairs: Dealer South : North-South vulnerable

Contract: 4♡
Lead: ◇Q

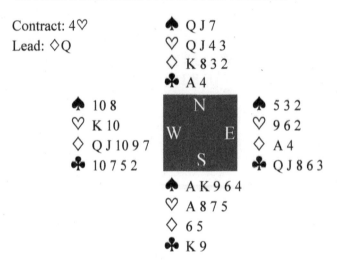

♠ Q J 7
♡ Q J 4 3
◇ K 8 3 2
♣ A 4

♠ 10 8
♡ K 10
◇ Q J 10 9 7
♣ 10 7 5 2

♠ 5 3 2
♡ 9 6 2
◇ A 4
♣ Q J 8 6 3

♠ A K 9 6 4
♡ A 8 7 5
◇ 6 5
♣ K 9

After ◇Q: two – four – five and ◇J: three – ace – six, East shifted to the ♣3. In an international pairs event, several declarers failed when they won the club switch and played ♡A and a second heart. West won and returned the ◇10. Dummy had to follow suit and East ruffed with the ♡9 to give the defence their fourth trick.

After trick 2, the diamond layout is known. The losing line could be foreseen. Win trick 3 with the ♣K and play a *low* heart. West can win with the ♡K and play another diamond, but if East ruffs, South can over-ruff and make the rest of the tricks routinely.

A low heart from hand works on any 3-2 split and caters for some 4-1 breaks. Short in diamonds, East might well have ♡K-10-6-2 or ♡K-9-6-2. If you start with ♡A and another heart, East comes to two trump tricks. If you play ♡5 and ♡9 or ♡10 from West, queen, king, you win any return from East and play ♡7 to the ♡J. If West shows out, you can finesse ♡8, cash ♡A for ten tricks.

You always count your cards face-down first and you always have 13, except on those occasions when you look at them first. That is when you hold 14.

41. Teams: Dealer East : Both vulnerable

```
              ♠ K 7 3
              ♡ A K 5 3
              ◇ K 7 2
              ♣ A Q J
                    N
              W           E
                    S
              ♠ A 4
              ♡ J 10 9 8 2
              ◇ A 6 3
              ♣ K 7 6
```

West	North	East	South
		Pass	1♡
Pass	2NT (1)	Pass	4♡ (2)
Pass	4NT (3)	Pass	5♡ (4)
Pass	6♡	All pass	

(1) Game-force, 4+ hearts
(2) Minimum opening, no shortage
(3) Key-card ask
(4) Two key cards for hearts, no ♡Q

West leads the ♣Q, taken by the ace. Hoping West might cover with the queen, South leads the ♡J, but West plays the ♡4. South rises with the ♡A. East plays the ♡7. South cashes the ♡K: six – eight – ♠2 from West. How would you continue?

41. Teams: Dealer East : Both vulnerable

Contract: 6 ♡   ♠ K 7 3
Lead: ♠Q   ♡ A K 5 3
                                 ◇ K 7 2
                                 ♣ A Q J

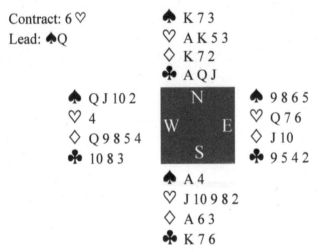

♠ Q J 10 2   ♠ 9 8 6 5
♡ 4   ♡ Q 7 6
◇ Q 9 8 5 4   ◇ J 10
♣ 10 8 3   ♣ 9 5 4 2

                  ♠ A 4
                  ♡ J 10 9 8 2
                  ◇ A 6 3
                  ♣ K 7 6

After ♠A, ♡A, ♡K, you are saddled with a heart loser. You cannot afford a diamond loser as well. Your only hope is that East has at most two diamonds. If so, you may be able to force East to give you a ruff-and-discard.

Do not play a third round of hearts yet. Cross to the ◇K and return a diamond. If holding a singleton diamond, East cannot afford to ruff the second diamond. After winning with the ◇A, cash ♠K and ruff dummy's third spade. Continue with three rounds of clubs and exit with a heart.

East wins and, out of diamonds, has to play a spade or a club. You discard a diamond from one hand and ruff in the other.

This play works just as well if East began with a void, a singleton or a doubleton club. If East ruffs a club after you have eliminated spades, East has to give you a ruff-and-discard. If East declines to ruff a club, you play a trump after the third club.

The only alternative to perseverance is failure.

42. Teams: Dealer North : East-West vulnerable

♠ A J 6 4 3
♡ J
♢ 9 8 7 6 4
♣ 10 5

♠ K 10 2
♡ A K 10 9 8 4 3
♢ A J
♣ Q

West	North	East	South
	Pass	3♣	4♡
Pass	Pass	Pass	

1. West leads ♣6: five – king – queen
2. East plays ♣A: ♡3 – ♣J – ♣10
3. South plays ♡A: five – jack – two
4. South plays ♡K: six – ? – ♣2. Your discard from dummy?
5. South plays ♡10: queen – ? – ♣3? Your discard from dummy?
6. West switches to the ♢K: ♢x – three – ace
7. South plays ♡9: seven – ? – ♣4. Your discard from dummy?

What next?

42. Teams: Dealer North : East-West vulnerable

Contract: 4 ♡
Lead: ♣6

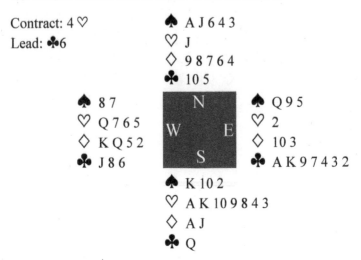

♠ A J 6 4 3
♡ J
♢ 9 8 7 6 4
♣ 10 5

♠ 8 7
♡ Q 7 6 5
♢ K Q 5 2
♣ J 8 6

♠ Q 9 5
♡ 2
♢ 10 3
♣ A K 9 7 4 3 2

♠ K 10 2
♡ A K 10 9 8 4 3
♢ A J
♣ Q

While removing West's trumps, South has to make three discards from dummy. Given East's 3♣ opening, the natural tendency is to place the ♠Q with West. If West has Q-x or Q-x-x in spades, you can make an overtrick by keeping four or five spades in dummy and discarding diamonds. However, your primary task at teams is to make your contract and not worry about an overtrick.

You can discard a spade and a diamond from dummy on the ♡K and ♡10. After West's defence, ♢K at trick 6, you can draw West's trump and pitch a spade or a diamond, as it happens, and play the ♢J. When the ♢10 drops, dummy's ♢9 will be high and you do not need to guess the spades.

It would be an error to discard three diamonds from dummy. Then after ♢K to the ace, draw the last trump and exit with ♢J, West wins and can continue diamonds, leaving you to guess the spades.

West should have defended better by playing the third club after winning with the ♡Q. Now you have a much tougher task.

We play Aspro discards. Partner's discards give me a headache.

43. Teams: Dealer East : East-West vulnerable

♠ K J 5
♡ K J 7 6
♢ 8 3
♣ A 9 7 6

♠ A Q 10 7 3
♡ 8 3 2
♢ A K
♣ K 5 3

West	North	East	South
		Pass	1NT (1)
Pass	2♣ (2)	Pass	2♠ (3)
Pass	4♠	All pass	

(1) 15-17 points
(2) 5-card major Stayman
(3) Five spades

1. West leads the ♣8: king – two – three
2. South plays the ♠5: four – ace – six

How would you continue?

43. Teams: Dealer East : East-West vulnerable

Contract: 4♠
Lead: ♠8

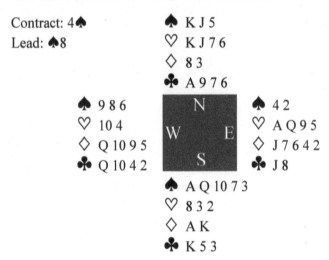

```
              ♠ K J 5
              ♡ K J 7 6
              ◇ 8 3
              ♣ A 9 7 6
♠ 9 8 6                      ♠ 4 2
♡ 10 4          N            ♡ A Q 9 5
◇ Q 10 9 5   W     E         ◇ J 7 6 4 2
♣ Q 10 4 2      S            ♣ J 8
              ♠ A Q 10 7 3
              ♡ 8 3 2
              ◇ A K
              ♣ K 5 3
```

Both follow to the second round of trumps and you have nine tricks on top. The extra trick could come from the clubs, but a 3-3 break is only about 36%. The chances in hearts are much better.

Should you draw the last trump before you play a heart? There is no need to do that. You would welcome a heart ruff, since it sets up dummy's fourth heart for a club discard.

Play a heart at trick 3: four – jack – queen. East can now beat you with a switch to the ♣8, but that would not happen in practice. At the table, East switched to a diamond. South won and now it was important to draw the last trump.

Then came the ♡8: ten – king – ace. South won the diamond exit and played the ♡3 to the ♡6 and ♡9. The ♡7 was now high for a club discard.

Roses are red but violets are wan,
Give yourself three chances instead of just one.

44. Teams: Dealer North : East-West vulnerable

♠ 7 2
♡ A K 4
◇ K Q J 6 2
♣ 8 5 3

♠ K Q J 10 9 5 3
♡ 6
◇ A
♣ K Q 4 2

West	North	East	South
	1◇	Pass	2♠ (1)
Pass	3◇	Pass	3♠ (2)
Pass	4♣	Pass	4NT
Pass	5◇ (3)	Pass	5♠
Pass	Pass	Pass	

(1) Strong jump-shift
(2) Sets spades as trumps
(3) One key card / one ace

West leads the ♡J. Plan the play.

44. Teams: Dealer North : East-West vulnerable

Contract: 5♠
Lead: ♡J

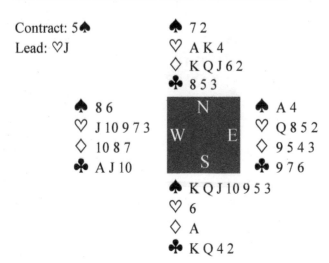

♠ 7 2
♡ A K 4
♢ K Q J 6 2
♣ 8 5 3

♠ 8 6
♡ J 10 9 7 3
♢ 10 8 7
♣ A J 10

♠ A 4
♡ Q 8 5 2
♢ 9 5 4 3
♣ 9 7 6

♠ K Q J 10 9 5 3
♡ 6
♢ A
♣ K Q 4 2

Without a heart lead, you could unblock the ♢A, cross to the ♡A
and take one discard on the ♡K and one on a diamond winner. If
you take the ♡A, discard a club on the ♡K and play a club, you
will lose a spade and two clubs.

You need to deal with the blockage in diamonds. The solution is
not difficult – after you see it, you will say, 'Of course' – but a
blind spot here is not uncommon.

Since you want to score diamond tricks, you win with the ♡A,
cash the ♡K and discard the blocking ♢A. Cash ♢K, ♢Q to
discard two clubs and then play a spade.

No brain is stronger than the weakest think. (Tom Masson)

45. Teams: Dealer East : Nil vulnerable

♠ K 6 3 2
♥ K J 6 5
⋄ K 8 4
♣ 7 6

♠ 9 7
♥ A Q 10 8 4 3
⋄ A J 7
♣ J 8

West	North	East	South
		Pass	1♥
Double	3⋄ (1)	Pass	4♥
Pass	Pass	Pass	

(1) Bergen raise: 10-12 points, 4+ hearts

West leads the ♣2: six – king – eight. East continues with the ♣A: jack – four – seven and switches to the ♠4: seven – ace – two. West returns the ♠Q: king – eight – nine.
Plan the play.

45. Teams: Dealer East : Nil vulnerable

Contract: 4♡
Lead: ♣2

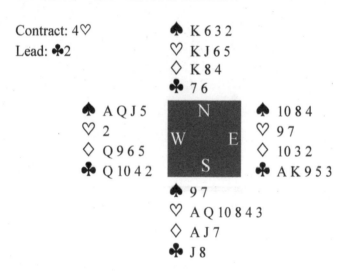

After winning ♣K and ♣A, East returned ♠4 to the ♠A. West's ♠Q was taken by the ♠K. If you are to amount to a strong bridge player, the first thing you should do on seeing dummy is to count dummy's points and your own. Dummy has 10 HCP, you have 12, total 22. Deducting from 40 means the opponents hold 18 HCP.

Apply that to this auction and the early play and you should know where the missing points are. East has shown up with 7 HCP. The other 11 will be with West (takeout double) and so finessing the ♢J is futile. With only 11 HCP, West figures to have four spades.

South should play ♡A, ♡K, spade ruff and run three more hearts. That leaves West with ♠J, ♢Q-9-6, dummy with ♠6, ♢K-8-4 and South with ♡8, ♢A-J-7. When South plays ♡8, pitching ♢4 from dummy, West must hold on to the ♠J, else dummy's ♠6 will be high. When West discards a diamond, South plays ♢K, ♢A, and the ♢J is high for South's tenth trick. Though it does not apply here, the squeeze works just as well if East has ♠J, ♢Q-x-x.

The unexamined life is not worth living. (Socrates)

46. Teams: Dealer East : Nil vulnerable

♠ A 9 4
♡ A 8 4
◇ A Q J 10 9
♣ K Q

♠ J 5 3
♡ K 6
◇ K 2
♣ A 10 9 6 4 3

West	North	East	South
		Pass	1♣
Pass	1◇	Pass	2♣
Pass	4♣ (1)	Pass	4◇ (2)
Pass	4NT	Pass	5◇ (3)
Pass	7♣	All pass	

(1) Sets clubs, asks for cue-bidding
(2) Shows the ◇K
(3) One key card for clubs

West leads the ♡3: ace – queen – six. Declarer plays the ♣K: two – three – eight and the ♣Q: five – four – ♡2. Plan the play.

46. Teams: Dealer East : Nil vulnerable

Contract: 7♣   ♠ A 9 4
Lead: ♡3   ♡ A 8 4
                               ◇ A Q J 10 9
                               ♣ K Q

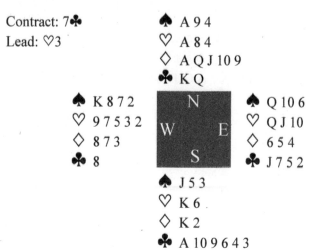

♠ K 8 7 2   N   ♠ Q 10 6
♡ 9 7 5 3 2   W   E   ♡ Q J 10
◇ 8 7 3   ◇ 6 5 4
♣ 8   S   ♣ J 7 5 2

                               ♠ J 5 3
                               ♡ K 6
                               ◇ K 2
                               ♣ A 10 9 6 4 3

When East turns up with four clubs to the jack, your knowledge of trump-reduction play is vital. You need to reduce your trumps to the same length as East's and then have the lead in dummy at trick 11. That will allow you to pick up East's trumps. You will need a little luck with East's side suits. You cannot afford East to have a singleton diamond, for example.

To bring your trumps down to two, the same as East now holds, you need to ruff twice in hand. At trick 4, cross to the ♡K, play the ◇K to the ◇A and ruff a heart. Follow up with the ◇2 to dummy and play two more diamonds to discard two spades. If East ruffs at any time, you over-ruff, draw East's last trump and return to dummy to cash the rest of the diamonds. If East has not ruffed in, ruff the fifth diamond yourself to come down to ♣A-10.

You have ♠J and ♣A-10 and East has ♠Q and ♣J-7. You play the ♠J to the ♠A. On the next spade, East has to ruff. You over-ruff and you have thirteen tricks. Lucky you were not in 7NT.

Reductio ad absurdum: To reduce your trump length and fail in your contract when drawing trumps would have worked.

47. Teams: Dealer North : North-South vulnerable

♠ K 8 6 5
♡ A J 3
◇ A 10 5
♣ 8 3 2

♠ A Q J 2
♡ Q 10 5
◇ J 4
♣ K 9 7 4

West	North	East	South
	1♣	Pass	1♠
2◇	2♠	Pass	2NT (1)
Pass	3♠ (2)	Pass	4♠
Pass	Pass	Pass	

(1) Inviting game, asking about North's trump length
(2) Four trumps, minimum opening

West leads the ◇K: ace – seven – four. Declarer plays the ♠K, ♠A and ♠Q. Both opponents follow to two spades. West discards the ◇2 on the third spade.

South plays the ♡Q: king – ace – four and cashes the ♡J and the ♡10, all following. South exits with the ◇J. West wins with the ◇Q and returns the ◇9: ten – ♡8 – ♣4.

You play the ♣2 from dummy and East plays the ♣Q. What do you play? If you have played low on the ♣Q, East continues with the ♣J. What now?

47. Teams: Dealer North : North-South vulnerable

Contract: 4♠   ♠ K 8 6 5
Lead: ◇K   ♡ A J 3
                      ◇ A 10 5
                      ♣ 8 3 2

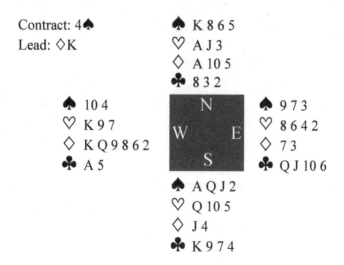

♠ 10 4   ♠ 9 7 3
♡ K 9 7   ♡ 8 6 4 2
◇ K Q 9 8 6 2   ◇ 7 3
♣ A 5   ♣ Q J 10 6

                      ♠ A Q J 2
                      ♡ Q 10 5
                      ◇ J 4
                      ♣ K 9 7 4

To be a good declarer, you need to count the opponents' hands.
You do this easily by noting when an opponent shows out of a suit
and deducing the number of cards in that suit each opponent held.

From the early play, you know West had only two spades and East
three. Each opponent followed to three hearts. East showed out on
the third diamond, discarding a heart. Therefore, West began with
six diamonds. You now know West's exact hand pattern: 2-3-6-2.

When you play a club from dummy and East plays the ♣Q, you
must play low. If you play the ♣K on the ♣Q and the situation is
as above, you lose three club tricks. When East continues with the
♣J, you should play the ♣K in case East has the ♣A (unlikely).

If the layout is as above it does not matter if you play a low club
or the ♣K. West wins and, with only diamonds left, has to give
you a ruff-and-discard.

*There are three types of bridge players. Those who can count and
those who can't.*

48. Teams: Dealer South : Nil vulnerable

♠ 10 8 7
♡ 9 4
◇ K J 7 5
♣ A Q 8 2

♠ A J 6
♡ K Q J 10 7 5 3
◇ Q 4 2
♣ ---

West	North	East	South
			1♡
1♠	Double (1)	Pass	3♡
Pass	4♡	All pass	

(1) For takeout, shows both minors

West leads the ♠K: seven – nine (high-encouraging) . . .
Plan the play.

48. Teams: Dealer South : Nil vulnerable

Contract: 4♡
Lead: ♠K

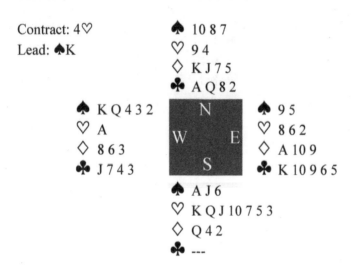

	♠ 10 8 7	
	♡ 9 4	
	◊ K J 7 5	
	♣ A Q 8 2	
♠ K Q 4 3 2		♠ 9 5
♡ A		♡ 8 6 2
◊ 8 6 3		◊ A 10 9
♣ J 7 4 3		♣ K 10 9 6 5
	♠ A J 6	
	♡ K Q J 10 7 5 3	
	◊ Q 4 2	
	♣ ---	

Even without West's 1♠ bid, you can foresee the spade ruff when East plays the encouraging ♠9 at trick 1. If you take the ♠A and play a trump, West wins, cashes the ♠Q and plays a third spade for East to ruff. One down when you lose the ◊A later.

It also does not help declarer if trick 1 goes ♠K: seven – nine – six. West continues spades, wins ♡A and gives East a spade ruff.

In the 1997 World Transnational Teams, Andrew McNair of Great Britain produced a neat deceptive play when he played the ♠J under the king at trick 1. Dropping the jack from A-J-x is usually seen only in a no-trump setting, but it worked perfectly here.

West naturally thought East had the ♠A – and who can blame West? – and played a low spade at trick 2. Declarer played dummy's ♠10, winning, and discarded the ♠A on the ♣A. Next came trumps and South lost only one spade and the two red aces.

In bridge, a deception lasts for merely a matter of minutes or seconds, but the satisfaction and appreciation of a successful deception can last for generations.

49. Pairs: Dealer South : East-West vulnerable

♠ A 6
♥ ---
♦ A 9 7 4 3
♣ J 10 9 7 4 2

♠ K 7 2
♥ Q 7 5 3 2
♦ 8
♣ A K 8 3

West	North	East	South
			1♥
Pass	1NT	Pass	2♣
Pass	6♣!	All pass	

As 5♣ is often a poor score at pairs, North jumped to 6♣. This carried some risk, but South had a suitable hand opposite.

West leads the ♠5. Plan the play.

49. Pairs: Dealer South : East-West vulnerable

Contract: 6♣

Lead: ♠5

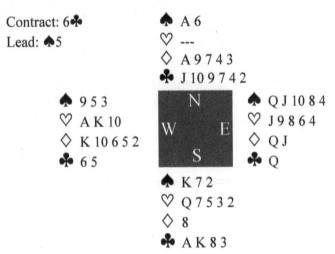

```
              ♠ A 6
              ♡ ---
              ◇ A 9 7 4 3
              ♣ J 10 9 7 4 2
  ♠ 9 5 3          N          ♠ Q J 10 8 4
  ♡ A K 10                    ♡ J 9 8 6 4
  ◇ K 10 6 5 2  W       E     ◇ Q J
  ♣ 6 5            S          ♣ Q
              ♠ K 7 2
              ♡ Q 7 5 3 2
              ◇ 8
              ♣ A K 8 3
```

The deal arose in the 2002 World Mixed Pairs. One possible line is to win trick 1 with the ♠K, cash the ♣A, ruff a heart, club to hand, ruff a heart. After ◇A, diamond ruff, heart ruff, South's ♡Q is high. South has 12 tricks via two spades, one heart, one diamond, two top clubs and six club ruffs. Twelve pairs in 6♣ made 12 tricks. That was worth 369/414 match points.

There were another sixteen pairs in 6♣ and each one made all the tricks via ♠A at trick 1, ◇A, diamond ruff, heart ruff, club to the ♣A, heart ruff, diamond ruff, heart ruff, diamond ruff, heart ruff, ♣J, ♠K, ♡Q. This line made two spades, one diamond, one heart, three ruffs in the South hand and six clubs in the North hand. Making thirteen tricks was worth 397/414 match points, an extra 6.7% for the overtrick.

Bridge players do it in Pairs.

50. Teams: Dealer North : North-South vulnerable

♠ A
♡ ---
◇ A Q 8 7 2
♣ A K Q J 7 6 3

♠ K Q 9 7 6 3
♡ K Q 10 5
◇ J 6
♣ 10

West	North	East	South
	2♣	Pass	2◇ (1)
Pass	3♣	Pass	3♠
Pass	4◇	Pass	4NT
Pass	5♠ (2)	Pass	6NT
Pass	Pass	Pass	

(1) Weak or waiting
(2) Three aces

Many would bid 2♠ as South after North's 2♣ opening, but that was not the system in use here.

West leads the ♡8: ◇2 – ♡A – ♡5. East switches to the ♣4. Plan the play.

50. Teams: Dealer North : North-South vulnerable

Contract: 2♠ doubled
Lead: ♡8

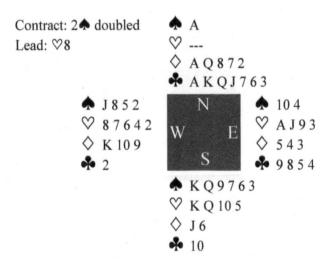

♠ A
♡ ---
◇ A Q 8 7 2
♣ A K Q J 7 6 3

♠ J 8 5 2
♡ 8 7 6 4 2
◇ K 10 9
♣ 2

♠ 10 4
♡ A J 9 3
◇ 5 4 3
♣ 9 8 5 4

♠ K Q 9 7 6 3
♡ K Q 10 5
◇ J 6
♣ 10

If East had returned a heart at trick 2, it would be plain sailing. Win ♡K and ♡Q, discarding two more diamonds from dummy, cross to the ♠A, return to the ♣10, cash the ♠K, discarding dummy's ◇Q, cross to ◇A and claim the rest of the tricks.

East's club return to your ♣10 makes it more awkward. Having discarded the ◇2 on the heart lead, South could discard two more diamonds on the ♡K, ♡Q and, when the ♡J has not appeared, finesse the ◇Q. On the actual layout, that works, but it is a poor line. If the finesse lost, East could also cash the ♡J for two down.

A little knowledge of jettison play allows you to make 6NT without requiring the diamond finesse. South wins the club switch with the ♣10 and cashes the ♡K, discarding the ♠A from dummy. Then the ♡Q, ♠K, ♠Q allow South to discard dummy's ◇7, ◇8, ◇Q, cross to the ◇A and claim twelve tricks.

One should always play fairly when one has the winning cards.
(Oscar Wilde)

A Bonus Puzzle:

Teams: Dealer West : Nil vulnerable

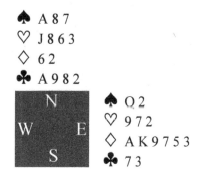

♠ A 8 7
♡ J 8 6 3
♦ 6 2
♣ A 9 8 2

♠ Q 2
♡ 9 7 2
♦ A K 9 7 5 3
♣ 7 3

West	North	East	South
1♠	Pass	1NT	Pass
2♣	Pass	2♦	2♡
Pass	Pass	2♠	Pass
Pass	3♡	All pass	

West leads the ♦10. How would you defend as East?

Teams: Dealer West : Nil vulnerable

Contract: 3♡
Lead: ◇10

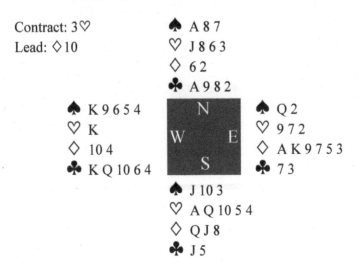

♠ A 8 7
♡ J 8 6 3
◇ 6 2
♣ A 9 8 2

♠ K 9 6 5 4
♡ K
◇ 10 4
♣ K Q 10 6 4

♠ Q 2
♡ 9 7 2
◇ A K 9 7 5 3
♣ 7 3

♠ J 10 3
♡ A Q 10 5 4
◇ Q J 8
♣ J 5

East won trick 1 with ◇K and shifted to ♠Q. That was unwise. As East had turned up with 9 HCP, South placed the missing points with West for the 1♠ opening. A heart to the ace brought its due reward and trumps were drawn. Declarer thus lost just one spade, two diamonds and a club for +140.

East has the ◇9 and so West's ◇10 is a singleton or top from a doubleton. Also counting points (nine in dummy, nine with East, ◇Q-J with South), West is likely to have ♡K or ♡Q singleton and will be able to win the third round of diamonds. The defence will still come to two tricks in the black suits for one down.

As East has a useful card via the ♠Q and nothing useful in clubs, the best carding for East is ◇A, ◇K and then the ◇9, all suit-preference for spades. West will ruff the third diamond with the ♡K, but with those powerful clubs, a switch to the ♣K is the normal move, despite East's signalling.

It is worse than a crime, it is a blunder. (Talleyrand)

You will not find the bonus problem in

50 Great Puzzles on Defence

by Ron Klinger

Weidenfeld & Nicolson
in association with
PETER CRAWLEY

but you will find fifty other entertaining and instructive puzzles on defence there (as well as a bonus puzzle there, too).